1. My Nature is Fire

My Nature is Fire

My Nature is Fire
Saint Catherine of Siena

CATHERINE M. MEADE, CSJ

ALBA · HOUSE   NEW · YORK

SOCIETY OF ST. PAUL, 2187 VICTORY BLVD., STATEN ISLAND, NY 10314

Library of Congress Cataloging-in-Publication Data

Meade, Catherine M.
   My nature is fire : Saint Catherine of Siena / by Catherine M.
  Meade.
      p.   cm.
   Includes bibliographical references.
   ISBN 0-8189-0615-4
   1. Catherine, of Siena, Saint, 1347-1380.   2. Christian saints-
-Italy — Biography.   I. Title.
   BX4700.C4M43   1991
   282'.092 — dc20   91-9224
                                              'CIP

Designed, printed and bound in the United States of
America by the Fathers and Brothers of the
Society of St. Paul, 2187 Victory Boulevard,
Staten Island, New York 10314, as part of their
communications apostolate.

Printing Information:

Current Printing - first digit   2 3 4 5 6 7 8 9 10 11 12

Year of Current Printing - first year shown

                                  1998

DEDICATED

to
My Aunt
the first Catherine in my life
and
to the memory of
My Father
whose love of learning remains an inspiration

TABLE OF CONTENTS

Preface ix
Introduction xiii

PART ONE
THE SACRED CANOPY

1. Siena: A Place and an Environment 3
2. The Church: Papacy, Clergy, and Faithful 35
3. The Medieval World View 57
4. The Autobiographical Resources 73

PART TWO
TO MIRROR THE TRINITY: CATHERINE'S INNER WORLD

5. Imagine a Circle with a Tree Sprouting in Its Center 89
6. Christ Has Made a Staircase of His Body 107
7. Every Good Work Is Done Through Your Neighbor 129

PART THREE
MY NATURE IS FIRE: THE PUBLIC FIGURE

8. Advising and Admonishing: A Hungry Longing for Peace 151
9. Holy and Constant Prayer: Mercy for the World 165

PREFACE

This reflection on the life and spirituality of Catherine of Siena stems from a deep conviction that knowing her can change one's life. Meeting Catherine produces an immediate recognition that here is someone who speaks from the experience of human struggle. Here is a woman whose deep interior prayer and lifelong effort to re-image herself in the likeness of her Creator led her to deliberate effort to effect change in her society. Perceiving the oneness inherent in the love of God, self, and neighbor caused Catherine to discern that contemplation promotes action; that is, to comprehend that the same unity binds an interior and outer life as well as private and public concerns. Catherine's harmonious view of life is a potential model for people who wish to confront the evils encountered in our age. Such then, is the value of Catherine of Siena's life: this woman's personal experience of God, profound in its simplicity, is powerful in its application to the world of her day and our own.

My background as an historian, together with my lived experience as a religious and a committed searcher for truth during all of my adult life, shapes the Catherine that I present in this reflection. Venturing to be taught by her own texts rather than by previous interpretations, I have chosen to concentrate on key symbols which offer access to Catherine's message. One who wishes to explore further will find much more in the entirety of her writing. *My Nature Is Fire* serves as an introduction to Catherine and her spiritual message.

In writing this study, I am reminded of the truism, attributed to Saint Bernard, that each generation stands on the shoulders of those who have gone before. Though I do not cite them in detail, I am aware of the tremendous debt that I owe to the many hundreds of men and women who have contributed to an understanding of this saint for more than six hundred years since her death. In my personal experience, I am additionally indebted to several who continue to reveal Catherine. Padre Giacinto d'Urso, O.P. and Karen Scott, Ph.D. of *Centro Culturale* at the monastery of San Domenico in Siena kindly diverted me from too obvious and precipitous conclusions. Suzanne Noffke, O.P. has provided me the freedom to explore Catherine's testament in translations of the *Dialogue, Prayers,* and one volume of *Letters* that are representative of the best of scholarship. Both she and I, in turn, are indebted to Giuliana Cavallini, O.P. whose 1968 Italian edition rescued the *Dialogue* from centuries of misconceptions which had negated its value as a personal experiential testament.

Naming all who encouraged me throughout the last five years would include many friends, colleagues, and students who demonstrated genuine interest and support. I must mention a few, however, whose conversation, patient reading, and criticism of portions of the manuscript have added immeasurably to its clarity: Sisters Viterbo McCarthy, Dorothy McKenzie, Agnes Melly, Rita McCormack, Mary Lou Cassidy, and Dr. Mary Bryan, together with the members of my writer's group Drs. Pamela Menke, Susan Nessen, Jane Roman, and especially Sister Margaret William McCarthy whose faith in this project has been continuous and unwavering. Sister Marie Cicchese edited the entire manuscript. The staff of the Regis College Library has been unfailing in courteous assistance.

On another level, this study would never have come to

completion without my nieces, Mary Doyle and Christine O'Brien, who word-processed the initial version of the manuscript until my colleague, Dr. Edward Stevens, introduced me to the mysteries of the computer. Neither would the project have been initiated without the opportunity offered through the Regis College sabbatical grant program during the academic year 1985-1986. The final product has been greatly enhanced by the cover design of Sister Mary Grace, O.P. (St. Dominic's Monastery, Washington, DC) and the illustrations by Mary Southard, C.S.J. (Spiritearth, Dover, MA).

In bringing the work to conclusion, I have been energized by the members of my religious community, the Congregation of the Sisters of Saint Joseph of Boston. Crucial to my perseverance has been the continuous enthusiasm and insightful wisdom of Leo Brassard, A.A. The contribution to my well-being by family and friends has made all the difference; in particular, I would like to mention my sister, Sister Maura Meade, S.N.D., who, although she did not live to see the work completed, remains an essential part of bringing the process to conclusion.

Catherine M. Meade, CSJ

Regis College
Weston, Massachusetts
March, 1991

ACKNOWLEDGMENTS

Excerpts from *Catherine of Siena: The Dialogue*, trans. by Suzanne Noffke, O.P. Copyright © 1980 by the Missionary Society of St. Paul the Apostle in the State of New York. Used by permission of Paulist Press.

Excerpts from *The Prayers of Catherine of Siena*, edited by Suzanne Noffke, O.P. Copyright © 1983 by Suzanne Noffke, O.P. Used by permission of Paulist Press.

Excerpts from *The Letters of St. Catherine of Siena*, Vol. 1, trans. by Suzanne Noffke, O.P. Copyright © 1988 by The Center for Medieval and Early Renaissance Studies, State University of New York at Binghamton. Used by permission of Medieval & Renaissance Texts and Studies.

Excerpts from *I, Catherine: Selected Writings of St. Catherine of Siena*, trans. by Kenelm Foster, O.P. and Mary John Ronayne, O.P. Copyright © 1980 by Kenelm Foster. Used by permission of William Collins Sons & Co. Ltd.

Excerpts from *Catherine of Siena as Seen in Her Letters*, trans. by Vida Scudder, copyright © 1927 by J.M. Dent & Sons Ltd. Used by permission.

INTRODUCTION

For those whose knowledge of Saint Catherine of Siena is minimal, one fact dominates their view of her, that she dared to speak openly before the Popes of her day. "What else did she do?" these people ask, instinctively doubting that one moment of confrontation could make a fourteenth century woman — or one of the twentieth century, for that matter — a canonized saint and a Doctor of the Church. After all, to be a saint requires perfect holiness of life while to be a Doctor of the Church demands a body of written work whose truth has withstood intense theological examination. In addition, each one of these titles suggests an acknowledgment accorded after death. Therefore, in the case of Catherine, it is fair to ask what gave her the right to speak out during her own lifetime. What accorded her the legitimacy that would make Popes listen? Furthermore, what in her life and writings still testifies to an authenticity that causes Christians to listen to her, even today? These questions create a framework for this study.

The life of Catherine of Siena — set down in the medieval hagiographical model of her fourteenth-century confessor, Raymond of Capua — provided answers for her own day. [1] Using a language and a mythology commonly understood by his society, Raymond rendered her — in the Latin terminology — *admiranda* rather than *imitanda*; he held her up for awe and reverence rather than presenting her in a way that might inspire others to imitate her. Raymond assumed that his readers understood his perspective because they, too, were immersed in his world view. For contemporary readers, however, Raymond's account distances Catherine from ordinary human life, providing little frame of reference applicable outside of the fourteenth century. Readers must look elsewhere for guidance to comprehend Catherine's integration of a deep inner spiritual life and an outer public one.

Fortunately, Catherine left a substantial self-revealing written legacy of three primary sources to instruct us about herself. During her active life, she dictated several letters a day; almost four hundred of these remain, containing applications of her spiritual teachings addressed to a multitude of individuals in a wide variety of circumstances. [2] A collection of twenty-six prayers, the majority dating from the period just prior to her death, allows insight into the concerns Catherine brought to prayer and permits a privileged access to her concept of Divinity. [3] The book length *Dialogue* is the mature fruit of her spiritual teaching written about three years before her death. [4] Taken together, these sources offer a rich combination of insights into Catherine's personality, her activities, and her inner journey.

The art of contemporary biography provides a methodology to apply this autobiographical evidence by suggesting three kinds of knowledge necessary for the evocation of a whole life. [5] First, biographers ask what is the context within which the subject lives out her life. How do the insights of her particular age and culture influence her development, her way of thinking, and her actions? Second, how does a particular person give shape and meaning to her life. How does she integrate the "manifest myth" — what the world observes — with the "secret inner myth" — the interior life upon which the public life depends? Third, what is the nature of the individual's struggle between "freedom" and "fate." What dynamic tension exists between her free choices and the unchangeable circumstances in which she makes them? Finally, good biography requires that these three kinds of knowledge be creatively integrated in the telling of a life story.

While making no pretense of being a full scale biography, the objective of this study is to provide insights into each of these three areas of knowledge about Saint Catherine of Siena. Part One explores the sacred canopy[6] of Catherine's life, the objective world of ideas and values created by her society, the world which she eventually confronted as a public figure. Part Two is the core of the study, taking the reader into the inner world of Catherine's mind and soul where, in solitary seclusion, she developed the unique spiritual way that empowered her to become an instrument of change in her time and place. Part Three examines the dual approach which Catherine took in her challenges to the Church and world of her day. Her letters to Pope Gregory XI — an example of her exterior language — are an apt illustration of the dramatic tension between Catherine's spiritual stance, her political philosophy, and the moral climate operative around her. Her prayer texts — Catherine's interior language — reveal her personal struggle between freedom and fate as she attempts to bring the objective reality of her outer world into harmony with her inner vision.

Catherine of Siena has much to teach a world that is increasingly concerned about survival. Living in an age as violent and threatened as our own, she demonstrates the critical value of inner resolve in responding to an uncertain future. Her spirituality of interior synthesis propelled her outward into the conflicts of what has been called the "calamitous fourteenth century"[7] to become a peacemaker, counselor, spiritual guide, and moral reformer in her medieval world. Though the clashing forces of her tumultuous world defied Catherine's efforts to stem their destructive tide, her valiant personal confrontation is worthy of examination.

Catherine anticipated the current value placed on interior wholeness when she emphasized the integration of her human faculties of memory, understanding, and will. In both the East and the West, much is being written about the enlightenment that flows from internal unity, seen as the door to mystical and contemplative union.[8] Today, spiritual teachers propose that every person has access to mystical enlightenment and that its realization comes through a unified grasp of one's interior self. Centuries ago, Catherine taught the same thing, that all can achieve the connective harmony leading to union with God, at whatever pace or intensity they choose and in whatever life circumstance they find themselves. There is, therefore, a universality to Catherine's spirituality that is relevant in every age.

Catherine's life exemplifies the strength of character and purpose which flows from the self-knowledge that is derived from the knowledge of God. She affirms that interior spiritual development inevitably moves one from self-concern to social consciousness. Transcending time with the universality of her story, Catherine demonstrates the drama of a David and Goliath in one person's inherent desire to change the world, however minutely. Her search for holiness, though exceptional, intense, and more profound than others, is so distinctly human that it offers to the world today a spirituality connected to human experience and translatable to every time and place.

ENDNOTES

1. *The Life of Saint Catherine of Siena (Legenda Major)*, trans. by George Lamb Kennedy, P.J. Kenedy & Sons, New York, 1960. Further citations from this source will be indicated in the text by L. followed by page references.

2. The letters available in English which will be quoted in this text are found in *Catherine of Siena as Seen in Her Letters*, ed. and trans. by Vida Scudder, Dutton, New York, 1927 (hereafter cited as Scudder); *I, Catherine: Selected Writings of Saint Catherine of Siena*, ed. and trans. by Kenelm Foster and Mary John Ronayne, O.P., Collins, London, 1980 (hereafter cited as *I, Catherine*); *The Letters of St. Catherine of Siena*, ed. by Suzanne Noffke, O.P., Vol. 52 of Medieval and Renaissance Texts and Studies, Binghamton, New York, 1988 (Vol. 1 of a projected four-volume edition, hereafter cited as *Letters*).

3. *The Prayers of Catherine of Siena*, ed. and trans. by Suzanne Noffke, O.P., Paulist Press, New York, 1983. Citations will be indicated in the text by P. followed by prayer number and page reference.
4. Catherine of Siena, *The Dialogue*, ed. and trans. by Suzanne Noffke, O.P., Paulist Press, New York, 1980. Direct citations will be indicated in the text by D. followed by chapter and page reference.
5. *The Biographer's Gift: Life Stories and Humanism*, ed. by James F. Veninga, Texas, A & M University Press, 1983. See Veninga, "Biography: The Self and the Sacred Canopy," pp. 59-79.
6. The "sacred canopy of environment" is a term created by the sociologist Peter Berger as a metaphor for the objective reality that humans create in a given time and place, the societal and cultural context in which an individual carries out his or her own personal struggle with "freedom" and "fate." Ibid., p. 66.
7. Barbara Tuchman, *A Distant Mirror*, Ballantine Books, New York, 1978, Foreword, xiii; for a detailed description of the difficulties of the years 1340-1380, see John Larner, *Italy in the Age of Dante and Petrarch, 1216-1380*, Longmans, 1980, pp. 256-265.
8. William Johnston, *Being in Love: The Practice of Christian Prayer*, Harper & Row, 1989, p. 55.

CHRONOLOGY

(numbers in parentheses refer to Catherine's age)

1347	Catherine is born on March 25 in Siena.
1353 (6)	She has a vision in which she feels called to a solitary and prayerful life.
1354 (7)	Catherine makes a private vow of virginity.
1354-62 (7-15)	Youthful period when Catherine demonstrates piety according to her knowledge of the lives of the saints. Raymond records what is reported by family and friends.
c. 1362-65 (15-18)	During these years, Catherine enters the beginning stage of an interior spiritual life. Self-knowledge grows within her knowledge of God and Catherine attends to the development of virtue.
1362 (15)	At the suggestion of Tommaso dalla Fonte, her first confessor, Catherine cuts off her hair in defiance of her family to prevent a marriage arrangement. Deprived of privacy within her home, she begins to retreat to the secret cell of her mind, discovering the cell of self-knowledge.
1363 (16)	Catherine publicly announces her intent never to marry. At her father's insistence, the family ceases to interfere, allowing her privacy for prayerful solitude and acts of piety.
1364-65 (17/18)	Catherine joins a Dominican third order of laywomen, the Mantellate, and makes private promises of poverty, chastity, and obedience.
c. 1365-68 (18-21)	These years, corresponding to Catherine's second spiritual stage, are marked by interior suffering, temptation, and purification. Catherine begins to leave solitude to serve her neighbor. She attracts followers, among them Bartolomeo Dominici, who becomes Catherine's friend, advisor, and second confessor.

c. 1369-74   These years correspond to the third stage of Catherine's
(22-27)   spirituality. Continuing to develop interiorly, she learns to
             live with conflict and criticism. As her active ministry ex-
             pands and her reputation grows, she experiences opposi-
             tion from the Friars and the Mantellate. Her lifestyle, her
             notoriety, and the prospect of travel outside of Siena are in
             question. During this time, Catherine experiences mystical
             death, symbolic of union with God. Her ministry of cor-
             respondence dates from this time.

1374 (27)   Catherine goes to Florence while the General Chapter of
             the Dominican Friars is convened there. Controversy over
             her public life is officially resolved when Raymond of Capua
             is assigned as her confessor.
             Another epidemic of the Black Death breaks out in Siena;
             Catherine and her followers spend the summer in the city
             tending the stricken.

1375 (28)   Catherine travels to Pisa to preach and teach; she uses the
             opportunity to encourage support for a papal crusade and to
             muster support for the papal league to prevent an Italian
             revolt against the papacy.

1376 (29)   Because of its anti-papal activities, Florence is placed under
             interdict. In April Catherine offers her services to this city
             as their mediator with Pope Gregory XI. She travels to
             Avignon, using the opportunity to urge the pope to return
             the seat of papal government to Rome. In September, when
             Gregory leaves Avignon for Rome, Catherine and her fol-
             lowers return to Siena.

1377 (30)   In May Catherine visits Rocca d'Orcia, outside Siena, to
             reconcile feuding families. Raymond is appointed prior of
             the Church of the Minerva in Rome. Catherine is isolated
             from papal affairs which are worsening throughout Italy. In
             October, she begins to dictate the *Dialogue*. By December,
             she is back in Siena continuing this work.

1378 (31)   At the request of Pope Gregory XI, Catherine goes to
             Florence as peace mediator, continuing to work on the
             Dialogue. At the death of Gregory in March, Urban VI is
             elected Pope. In September, the election of a second

pontiff, Clement VII, initiates the great schism which will dominate Church politics until the mid-fifteenth century. In early August, when peace is restored between Florence and Pope Urban VI, Catherine returns to Siena where she completes the *Dialogue* in October. In November, at the request of Urban, Catherine takes up residence in Rome to support the Urbanist cause.

1379 (32)   In Rome, Catherine works on behalf of unity and reform in the Church, writing letters, praying, and offering her own body in expiation. She and a group of disciples form a community which practices charity among the needy. Many of the *Prayers* date from this period.

1380 (33)   In February, Catherine is confined to bed. Her death follows in April.

My Nature is Fire

PART ONE

THE SACRED CANOPY

Contemporary biographers place a rightful significance on "a sense of place as a shaper of character."[1] For Catherine, Siena was the intimate locale in which she became a person, providing childhood impressions which shaped her solitary inner world. Within the protecting circle of Sienese communal life, Catherine's development was equally influenced by her relationships with important persons and groups such as her family, her neighborhood, and her local church.[2] Thus, an investigation of these aspects of Catherine's formative experience will illuminate the foreground of her "sacred canopy of environment."

Within the intimate circle of family, Catherine experienced anger, discord, opposition, and alienation which were challenging deterrents to the development of a harmonious inner life. In the public realm of the neighborhood and the city, her alternate family, Catherine found warmth, acceptance, and a liberal education in the accepted social, political, and religious ideas of her time. In Catherine's case, it is possible to document additional sources: the Dominican friars who directed her religious education, texts which contained the elements of her contemporary spirituality, and political paintings which summarized medieval beliefs about good government. Catherine relied on these formative medieval influences as she struggled to grasp the meaning of her life call. The historic appellation, Catherine of Siena, rather than Catherine Benincasa, attests to her total identification with her city in a period when the urban experience was celebrated as the peak of societal development.

1

SIENA: A PLACE AND AN ENVIRONMENT

Perched on the crest of three high ridges from which deep valleys drop abruptly to the surrounding plains, Siena today remains relatively unchanged from Catherine's day. Visitors to this Tuscan hill town are instantly drawn back more than six hundred years to her medieval milieu. Stout buildings line steeply inclined, deeply shadowed, walled passages that emerge at intervals into open spaces awash with bright sunlight. At one such spot, a wall marker and painting indicate that Catherine, five or six years of age, had a vision of Jesus Christ in a majestic bridal chamber which appeared in the sky across the valley high above the craggy rise crowned by the Church of Saint Dominic.

Returning from her sister's home, she climbed the steep and narrow Via di Valle Piatta and turned downward into the Via del Costone to the edge of a sheer precipice. Here, where the Via del Costone angles sharply right before dropping into the Fontebranda Valley, an inscription states that Catherine saw Christ seated on an imperial throne dressed in papal attire, with a tiara on his head. In the company of the apostles Peter, Paul, and John, Christ smiled lovingly on her with eyes full of majesty, raised his right hand over her and made the sign of the cross to give her a priestly blessing. (L. 25) In accounts of the life of Catherine of Siena, this childhood vision identifies her as a potential mystic who has direct contact with God.

Throughout the city, cascades of golden-colored dwellings topped with red-orange clay roofs flow over the hills and down into the valleys below. Squealing masses of black swallows dart, circle, and swoop continuously up, down, and over the rooftops while flocks of resident pigeons flutter noisily from the scaffolding holes in the walls or from overhanging eaves. Human noises of city life compete with nature as children call and cry out at play. Housewives can be heard singing at their work or scolding loudly while pedestrian voices, amplified in the deep walled streets and passageways, echo and reverberate across the city like responses of a cacophonous chorus. Bells, tolling from the churches, call the devout to worship and mark the passing hours, rising to jubilant crescendo at the major turning points of the day. Stirred by this ringing cadence, the birds rush and swoop with even greater intensity, adding to the ritual which marks the daily passage of time.

The six centuries that have passed since Catherine Benincasa grew up in Siena fade away when we read of her time:

> Life in the Italian walled-in city of about 1300 went on in a tight world of personal relations and public settings. Gossip and rumor rippled back and forth across the warp and woof of close family ties, inherited family friendships and animosities, numerous street acquaintances, and peripheral contacts that were endlessly being renewed. . . .
>
> Sounds . . . were . . . conducted by the habitat of the city, where narrow streets, lying between high stone constructs amplified noises and smells, quarrels and conversations. . . .
>
> No urban Italian could escape the eyes and curiosity, and almost the very need to know, of his neighbors. [3]

Allusions to cities in Catherine's writings make it clear that she was deeply affected by the elements of city structure, its life, and function, as well as the political realities of everyday government. That she knew her own city of Siena well is also obvious. As a small child, she frequently visited her sister's home, travelling deep into the Fontebranda Valley, up over the crest of the hill which supported the Cathedral, and down again into the next valley. In later years, she chose a similar route to reach the Santa Maria della Scala Hospital opposite the Duomo to visit and to nurse the sick and dying. During the last plague epidemic of 1374, she and her followers were familiar figures on the streets and passageways throughout the city as they comforted the dying and buried the dead.

Medieval people lived as much in the streets as in their homes; open archways, balconies, and exterior staircases provided ready access between private and public places so that family life was scarcely separated from life in the extended family of the neighborhood. Like most Sienese, therefore, Catherine was a child of her city as much as of her family; the objective reality of the world around her was text and teacher to her observant and inquiring mind.

In a psychological as well as a physical sense, Catherine's Sienese environment was communal. Physical closeness, produced by natural proximity and architectural structure, was an external indication of a society whose goals were corporate rather than individualistic. This commingling of personal and public life expectations was a formative reality uniquely medieval and quite foreign to contemporary experience. [4] The communal government of a late medieval Italian city-state assumed direction of a wide range of services integrating political, social, religious, and economic necessities. Civic duties included tasks of a religious nature such as the building and beautification of church property, the maintenance of hospitals, the provision for public charity, and the regulation and celebration of religious holy days. Growing up with this notion of civic governance in which the religious and the political enjoyed equal and frequently overlapping prerogatives predisposed Catherine to perceive her future religious calling as a natural fusion of spiritual and worldly necessities.

Commerce and banking generated the lively financial climate

which characterized the thriving medieval urban center of Siena in Catherine's day. Lavish craft work by jewelers and goldsmiths made the city an important stop on the trade routes, increasing its wealth and economic activity. Residing along the crests of the three hills, prosperous citizens dominated the political and economic climate while the less affluent and poor lived in dwellings which cascaded down the hills into the deep valleys. In one of these, the Fontebranda, the Benincasa home stood slightly below the crest.

The non-noble class, comparable to a later bourgeoisie, were known as the *popolo*. Led by successful merchants, manufacturers, and bankers, they had succeeded in wresting political control of the commune from the hands of the ancient nobility by 1280. As members of the *popolo*, the Benincasa men enjoyed a limited sense of participation, appropriate to their middle-class wealth, in the governance of their city. Hence, family conversation would include not only the status of the cloth trade but also the daily social and political activities of a city growing ever more organized and beautiful. Under the direction and administration of the wealthier and more powerful members of the *popolo*, led by the ruling Nine, [5] Siena became, in the early fourteenth century, a prime example of the maturity of medieval urban life achieved in the later middle ages. [6]

In the reorganization and decoration of public urban space, every aspect of urban life was addressed. An enlargement of the Cathedral, the communal focus of religious presence; the construction of the Palazzo Pubblico, the seat of civic power; and the development of the Campo, the central market space — all proceeded apace. [7] Reorganization and improvement of streets connecting all parts of the commune preceded the provision for a public water supply in the heart of the Campo. This last was considered the crowning achievement of a medieval urban civilization. Campo and Palazzo Pubblico both bear the stamp of the ruling Nine who initiated them; repeated references to three, the *terzi* or three historic sections of the city, and nine, the multiple of three which made up the leadership, appear in their decoration and symbolism.

Opportunity for employment in public works drew migrant workers from the countryside into the city in such numbers that the population within the city walls peaked just before the Black Death epidemic of 1348 to a new density of approximately 50,000.[8] This activity created a sense of prosperity, of well-being, and of the harmony that should exist in a city well governed by dedicated citizens. Together with these positive effects, however, came the heightened stresses associated with urban congestion: shortages of food, housing, and living space. Unfortunately, the Black Death resolved these last crises by halving the population; it also slowed considerably the pace of the public works program.

It is likely that Catherine, an independent yet highly introspective and sensitive child, would react positively to the beauty and harmony of her city; venturing into the streets, she would be affected by her environmental surroundings. Modern theories of public space hold that sensitivity to environmental surroundings can engender a sense of self and self-confidence, a sense of safety, and a sense of being in scale with one's surroundings, of being the right size.[9] Catherine, as any small child, would respond to openness and security, to the warmth, activity, noise, color, size, and shape which Siena, with its warm and inviting winding and circular street pattern, provided.

Streets feeding from all sections of the city led to the central Campo, a public space considered more harmonious and beautiful than any other in Italy. Centuries of flowing rain water from three high ridges had created an open area forming this central, low-lying, historically neutral space. Shaped like an inverted shell or a fan, to some the Campo represented the enveloping mantle of the Virgin who protected Siena. The reddish, burnt Siena, herringbone brick floor, divided into nine sectors by strips of white stone, sloped downward to converge in a single point before the impressive symbol of city government, the Palazzo Pubblico. Repetition of the delicately columned triple bayed window pattern of this public building on all the private palaces facing the Campo, evoked the atmosphere of a large amphitheater. Indeed, both acoustically and physically, the Campo did and still does serve this purpose on public occasions.

In Catherine's day, the daily morning market activity took place here, so the noise and bustle of buyers and sellers, reverberating from the encircling curtain wall of buildings, added a welcoming rhythm of warm acceptance to one who idly wandered into the scene in search of excitement or came on the serious business of doing errands for a busy mother. Attractive as this morning activity and noisy good spirits might be, the quiet calm of afternoon and early evening in the Campo, restful in muted shadows, also welcomed a child of Catherine's introspective nature.

In beautifying the Campo, the governing Nine created a center of civic pride; a Sienese chronicler recorded their success in 1347, the year of Catherine's birth:

> The Campo of Siena was finally completed. It is held to be
> one of the most beautiful of all squares which can be seen
> not only in Italy but in the whole of Christendom. . . .[10]

The entire Campo became a symbolic representation of love for the city to replace divisive loyalties to clan, family, and neighborhood voluntarily abandoned by submission to the rule of a unified commune.[11]

The structural focus of this civic oneness and of the Campo itself was the Palazzo Pubblico. Its adjacent bell tower, the Torre della Mangia, completed in the year of Catherine's birth, rose 283 feet into the sky. This slender reddish brick shaft should have appeared awkward and out of balance with the low stout civic center; instead, like a cathedral campanile, it achieved magnificence. Because of its height, the tower had an enduring function in the life of the Sienese people. Visible from all quarters of the city, it drew people to the Campo like a magnet and gave rise to the adage that to be Sienese was to be born in the shadow of "the *Mangia.*"[12] From its grey stone crenelated belfry, the bell rang out the significant hours to dictate the daily civic life of the commune; each morning and evening it tolled the curfew which opened and closed the city gates.

On the lofty eminence of the edge of the Castelvecchio, the highest ground in the city, the Cathedral, its vast dome resting on the huge black and white marble walls of the central nave, dominated the skyline of Siena. Its marble banded campanile stood sentinel to this religious heart of the commune. In Catherine's day, the Cathedral had not yet achieved the grandeur of today though its elegance and opulence was more than representative of the period.

The Cathedral piazza of Catherine's time contained that subtle medieval combination of the "word" and the "deed": the Cathedral where the word of God was preached, and opposite it, the hospital where the word might be translated into deeds of charity toward one's neighbor. Later in Catherine's life, the hospital of Santa Maria della Scala became for her a place of the "deed," where she served her neighbor who was in need. Today, a chapel beneath the hospital, the Cappella della Notte, commemorates the nights that she spent there with her followers when the curfew required her to remain out of the street until the morning bell.

Looming above the Fontebranda valley, the Cathedral was clearly visible from the Benincasa home. Behind the family residence the yellow tinted raw Siena structure of the Church of San Domenico, spare and strikingly vertical, crowned the height of the Camporeggio. Unlike the Cathedral, San Domenico, the headquarters of the Dominican Order in Siena, was of plain material, sparse in decoration, yet expansive in length, width, and height. Its deep open interior well was designed for the work of the "preaching friars" as the Dominicans were then known, waiting to be filled with the word of God, a word which spoke of simplicity of life founded on Gospel poverty. The contrasting styles of the Dominican Church and of the Cathedral represented the extremes of the religious mood of Catherine's day: simplicity versus grandeur and emotional spirituality versus authoritarianism.

The Family Setting

The deep narrow crevasse of the Fontebranda Valley, dropping sharply from the high ground of the Castelvecchio where the Cathedral stood, rose just as abruptly to the height of the Camporeggio and the Church of San Domenico. Nestled into the sloping hillside below was the Benincasa home, overshadowed by the two churches whose bells competed noisily as they reverberated across the valley. From childhood, this family setting influenced Catherine's sense of the dominating religious presence in her city. Its position part way into the valley also dictated her social and political formation. Above, the city of medieval grandeur bustled with the activity of trade, banking, and political ferment; below, the equally dynamic commotion of ordinary living and practical occupations energized the atmosphere of the neighborhood.

The lower valley housed the leatherworkers; the smell of tanning operations wafted upward to mingle with the aroma raised by dye-making, the Benincasa family trade. The fountain of the Fontebranda, focus of the perennial need of water for life and work, drew citizens down into the valley to this common meeting place with daily regularity. To envision Catherine coming of age in this busy and communal milieu of continuous work and activity is to understand what research in medieval urban social patterns and structures suggests; that is, the wider communal family of the neighborhood participated fully in a child's development. Stories in the *Legenda* support this theory of medieval life. Catherine's mother, Lapa, recalling Catherine as a particularly pleasant and attractive child, told Raymond that neighbors used to carry her home with them to enjoy "her playfulness and childish prattle." (L. 23) Inter-familial relationships were taken for granted in this close knit society. Since neighbors shared communally in child rearing, they felt free to engage in discussion of each other's children as they grew to maturity; hence, Catherine's reputation for holiness first came to public knowledge through them. Every aspect of her unusual behavior would be of interest because saintliness intrigued all medieval people. The presence of a holy person in their midst had social consequence as many were drawn by the aura of power that emanated from them. [13]

This open ambience of the neighborhood gains significance in light of the character of the Benincasa household. When Catherine was born into the large and comfortably prosperous working class family of Giacomo and Lapa Benincasa on March 25, 1347, she was the next to the last of twenty-five children. Her extended family comprised a crowded and bustling household whose composition was constantly growing and changing as, according to custom, the older sons and their wives raised the next generation in the parental home. (L. 44) Necessarily large to accommodate this inter-generational arrangement, the Benincasa house also contained the family work area where the men made and mixed dyes for linen or woolen cloth. (L. 21) Lapa described two long flights of stairs from the front door to the attic. (L. 58) Though Raymond recorded that the family was of "a highly respectable class and enjoyed a considerable degree of comfort," (L. 19) their fortunes were entering a period of adversity during Catherine's youth, increasing the necessity of the arrangement of an influential marriage for her.

Obviously worn out by repeated pregnancies and domestic demands, Lapa was, nevertheless, a forceful and dominant person in her household. According to neighbors who reported to Raymond, she was prone to emotional outbursts directed to her husband and her children. Sometimes, they said, she "went on and on, wailing and shrieking" so that the "whole neighborhood was often roused by Lapa's cries and there would be a rush to see what new misfortune had befallen her." (L. 58) Catherine's vocation was undoubtedly influenced by the unrest in Lapa's home; certainly, her personality development was.

She learned early to meet her mother's sharp tongue and controlling behavior with exterior calm and strength, though probably not without inner trepidation. A contest of wills continued throughout their lifetimes. In this letter to her mother dated 1376, written while she was on her return journey from Avignon, Catherine attempted to reason with her mother who complained continuously about her absence:

> Like a good sweet mother, you must rest content and not be disconsolate, bearing the burden for God's honor, and for your own salvation and mine. I remember that you did this for temporal goods, when your sons were leaving you to acquire temporal riches. Yet now, when the stake is eternal life, you find it so burdensome that you say you will fade away if I don't answer quickly! . . . Be comforted for the love of Christ crucified instead of thinking you have been abandoned by God or by me. [14]

By the time Raymond tapped this mother's memories of a child whom she had never understood and who had resisted her every effort at direction and control, Lapa was eighty years old. Her age and the fact that she had lived to see Catherine publicly acclaimed a saint undoubtedly colored her recollections. She confessed to a special love for her because she had nursed her until she was ready to be weaned, something she had been unable to do with her other children. (L. 22) Incidents, very ordinary for a medieval child attracted by stories of saints, such as playing games of prayer and bodily flagellation with her little friends became *admiranda* in the mother's telling. A typically childish practice of visibly praying on every step became a miraculous event of levitation, preserved in one painting based on the legend. [15] In another, what was probably her father's sense of a spiritual aura, perceived when he observed his child in prayer, in Lapa's recounting became an objective image, a white dove flying around her head.

Giacomo Benincasa, Catherine's father, was reserved, restrained, and quietly controlled in the midst of the household ferment, "a man honest in all things, without deceit or guile, free from evil, fearing God." (L. 12) He, too, professed a special love for his holy daughter, which grew to respectful admiration. At first, he joined in the family punishment of Catherine, designed to force her to forget her dreams of sanctity and submit to a favorable marriage arrangement, but he eventually took control and ordered his wife and sons to stop their harassment. "From now on," Raymond quotes him as saying, "let no one upset this my dearest daughter or dare to interfere with her. . . ." (L. 45, 49)

Catherine had a warm relationship with Bonaventura, her favorite sister, who married when Catherine was six. Bonaventura's unhappiness in the early years of her marriage obviously remained fresh in Catherine's mind because she recounted it to Raymond some twenty years later. (L. 20) When Catherine was ten, it was only Bonaventura who could weaken her determination against marriage, prevailing upon her to submit to some of the local courting customs such as washing her neck, bleaching her hair, and making herself visible to potential suitors by lingering in the doorway. (L. 36-38) In the midst of these preparations, Bonaventura died while giving birth; immediately, Catherine confronted her family with renewed determination to lead a solitary, celibate, and consecrated life.

Catherine's brothers, engaged in the family business, were angered by her stubborn evasion of the marriage arrangement which they considered essential to recoup the family financial position. (L. 42-44) Being older and male, they appeared to share in the parental decision making and joined in the family plan to discipline Catherine until Giacomo commanded them to desist and to allow her to live prayerfully in seclusion within the family circle. Since the brothers and their wives were raising families in the household, there were always young babies around; many incidents give evidence of the affection Catherine had for these children. A sister-in-law, Lisa, who shared the Benincasa family life became a devoted companion as well as a Mantellate after her husband's death. Her memories enliven Raymond's presentation of these early years. (L. 56)

When the family business failed after 1368, Catherine's brothers took up residence in Florence. From a rather sharp letter written to one of them, we gain additional insight into the dynamics of the Benincasa family relationships:

Let me also remind you of the need to make amends for your ingratitude and lack of feeling. I mean your debt to your mother, whom you have a God-given duty to honor. I have watched your ingratitude increasing to the point that not only have you not supported her as you should have done (let's grant that you are excused for this because you are not able) — but even if you had been able I am not sure that you would have done so, for you've been mean even with words. What ingratitude! You forget her labor in bringing you into the world, the milk with which she fed you, and all the trouble she had in rearing you and the others. You may want to say that she didn't look after us, but I say that isn't true. Her great care and concern for you and your brother have cost her dearly. And even if it were true, you are still the one who is under an obligation to her, not she to you. She did not get her flesh from you, but gave you hers. [16]

Research into the social ramifications of sanctity in medieval society corroborates that family conflict and turmoil inevitably followed from a youth's choice of an ascetic lifestyle. Catherine was only one of many such medieval children who exhibited extreme patterns of youthful sanctity, and Lapa only one among many mothers who looked on in dismay as her child withdrew more and more into solitude, self denial, and self-inflicted corporal punishment. (L. 56) One study concludes that for female children, seven was the common year for the manifestation of religious impulses; that celibacy was central to a decision since arranged marriages occurred so early; that the family was the first context in which the child's independence and determination was tested; and that most parents reacted with alarm to the ascetic practices of their holy children. [17] Success in the pursuit of medieval holiness depended on "sheer force of personality," and for the female child of this era, "temptation, self-doubt, disbelief, scorn, and persecution were the crucible in which her will was tempered and tested." [18] In Catherine's case, these conclusions are borne out by our information about her familial setting.

Religious Life and Practice

The white habited Dominican friars with their flowing black outer cloaks were familiar figures on the streets and lanes of Catherine's neighborhood. From Raymond's descriptions it is obvious that the friars had some fascination for her and played meaningful roles in her life and that of her family. It was to a Dominican that Giacomo and Lapa went for guidance when they were troubled by Catherine's obstinacy in opposing their arrangements for her marriage. Her first confessor, Fra Tommaso dalla Fonte, orphaned during the 1348 plague epidemic, lived as a young man in the Benincasa home where his Dominican vocation was nurtured. When Catherine felt called to serve God in a special way, she not only sought his guidance, but was herself drawn to the Dominican way of life.

The monastery adjoining the Church of San Domenico in Catherine's day was typical of Dominican foundations; fundamentally, it was, by rule, a house of studies even though it was far removed from the great centers of learning such as Paris and Bologna, and even from the more cosmopolitan city of nearby Florence. Custom dictated that one friar within the monastery be designated as resident preacher, responsible for dogmatic instruction in faith and morals. On great feasts and during the prime liturgical seasons such as Lent and Advent, a reputed friar from another monastery would be invited to preach. In addition, Dominican monasteries had a resident *lettore* or director of studies in each priory to supervise the principal activity of the Order, study and preparation for preaching. Since Siena was such a small establishment, this was not always possible, but in Catherine's time, two of her learned associates filled this position: Raymond of Capua and Bartolomeo Dominici. [19]

As a child, Catherine received the catechetical instruction typical for her age; she learned the creed and the commandments, was instructed regarding the capital sins, the theological and cardinal virtues, and was prepared to receive the sacraments. Beyond the elementary level of childhood catechetical instruction, information and religious inspiration came from the ordinary preaching and instruction that was part of the regimen of Dominican parish life. Once she began to gain a reputation for sanctity, Dominican influence became exclusive as she was forbidden by them to attend other churches. [20]

Later, when Catherine joined the lay third order of the Sisters of Penance of Saint Dominic, she followed the requirements of the order: attending the morning liturgy at San Domenico, frequenting the sacrament of Penance, and receiving the Eucharist when permitted. Instruction in the tertiary rule was provided on the first Friday of each month by the Dominican spiritual director assigned to the Sisters.[21] Since the friars were dedicated to and thoroughly prepared for the apostolate of preaching, the quality of religious education attained through this means would be high by medieval standards; in addition, Catherine profited from individual counsel and conversation with many of the friars. Some of the emphases of Dominican spirituality which seem to have influenced Catherine were its stress on penance, fasting, abstinence, and the use of an instrument of physical discipline.[22] Dominican teaching which was theocentric and Christological in its focus on God, Christ, the Crucifixion, the Sacred Heart, the Precious Blood, the Name of Jesus, and the Mother of God, also accented loyalty to the Church and to the Pope.

Membership in the Mantellate, the popular name of the Sisters of Penance, placed Catherine directly under Dominican authority. Theoretically, the Sisters were responsible to the Master General of the Order, but in practice, the provincial superior appointed as immediate director a local friar who was responsible for calling monthly meetings, presiding at the election of a prioress, celebrating Mass for the group, preaching for them, and interpreting their rule.[23] He had complete authority to correct penitents who transgressed or neglected the rule as well as a fair amount of control over their freedom of action; for example, no Mantellate could travel outside her city without his express permission.

Members promised obedience to him and to the prioress, a promise which became problematic for Catherine when her reputation grew and public demands for her presence outside of Siena placed her at variance with more conservative, and/or jealous, friars and sisters. (L. 363-364) She and her followers were then placed under the direct supervision of Raymond of Capua, first by the Master General of the Order and later by Gregory XI in an official papal bull. They were thus freed from the myopic focus of the Sienese group but were still subject to the Church through a very definite chain of command.

Entrance to and profession in this third order followed a pattern similar to that of the friars; during a probationary period, the candidate was vested with a habit to the accompaniment of prayers, blessings, and hymns in the presence of the male Dominican community. At the end of the probationary period, a permanent profession was made which obliged the member to live according to the rule until death. This rule included the daily recitation of the canonical hours of the Church, together with confession and communion on the four main feasts of the liturgical year: Christmas, Easter, Pentecost, and either Mary's Assumption or her Nativity. More frequent communion was allowed with permission. Though no formal canonical vows were taken, the evangelical counsels of poverty, chastity, and obedience, modeled on the values taught by Christ in the Gospels and exercised by the friars, stimulated many to a deeply religious way of life.

Under Dominican influence, Catherine was steeped in the prevailing spirituality of the time, that of Saint Augustine. Dominic, an Augustinian Canon prior to his founding of the Order, adapted the Rule of Augustine for his foundation; the Rule of the Mantellate, therefore, emphasized an Augustinian spirituality of interiority. Augustinian thought pervaded the Dominican sermons which she heard; in addition, since her Dominican disciple Tommaso d'Antonio translated Augustine's discourses into the vernacular Tuscan Italian, they were readily available to her. While the principles of the *Summa* of the Dominican Thomas Aquinas (c. 1225-1274), also grounded in Augustinian thought, had not yet predominated medieval theology, they would be familiar to Catherine from the teaching and conversation of her learned Dominican associates. [24]

Catherine was familiar with and later adapted in her own writings symbolic representations of the spiritual life familiar in her day: the "Bridge" and the "Tree of Virtue" of Saint Gregory the Great, [25] the tree of life of Ubertino, [26] and the iconographic imagery of the cross as tree or ladder dating back to the *Vexilla Regis* of Fortunatus in the fifth century. The trinitarian emphasis in her own teaching which linked the three interior human faculties of memory, understanding, and will with the divine Trinity indicated her familiarity with Augustine's *de Trinitate*, the earliest formal exposition of this mystery to link the human and the divine in this manner. [27]

Quotations in her writings reveal a deep knowledge of scripture and of the major texts of medieval writers although the way in which they are used disclose a dependence on an aural familiarity from homilies and conversation. [28] Her acquaintance with scripture, impressive for the depth of its contemplative integration into her life and thought, is clearly informed by a medieval rendering in dialect, [29] and a free interpretation flowing from repeated meditation on a remembered text.

Several writers and preachers of the time influenced Catherine's piety and thought. We know that she had read the popular treatises of the Dominican, Domenico Cavalca, and stories of Saint Dominic and other Dominican saints. [30] Like other spiritual writers of his day, Cavalca (1270-1342), esteemed as one of the fathers of Italian prose, was apt to tell the same stories as the myths and legends in a vivid and colorful manner that had "more power to move the heart than most modern romances." [31] Cavalca was most noted for translations of lives and legends of the fathers and early saints of the Church. [32] If these were the renditions of holy lives which formed Catherine's childish impression of sanctity, her struggles to be "holy" become understandable since in Cavalca's subjects abstinence and patience predominate. His saints always emerge victorious in the struggle with self; his emphasis is always on the victory rather than the human cost in the struggle.

Catherine also became acquainted with heroic saints popular in her day through a medieval collection of the lives of the saints, *The Golden Legends* of the Dominican friar, Jacobus de Voragine (c. 1228-1298).[33] The legends were appealingly simple stories collating the lore of tradition regarding a saint, adding a wealth of personal, often apocryphal, detail appealing to the medieval imagination. Widely used in the Church for readings to commemorate saints on their name days, the *Golden Legends* illustrated the heroic virtue of the early saints with a miraculous quality. Two of these, Catherine of Alexandria and Mary Magdalene, were especially dear to Catherine.

According to the *Golden Legends*, Catherine of Alexandria, an early Christian who won the "crown of martyrdom," confounded pagan scholars assigned to interrogate her with the "keenness of her mind" and the depth of "her wisdom and philosophy." A wheel, constructed for her torture, fell apart in response to her prayers. Deprivation of food had no effect, as Christ, her spouse, sent an angel to feed her. After she was beheaded, her body exuded milk rather than blood, while later her undecayed bones, removed to Mount Sinai by a faithful follower, issued a healing oil.[34] This saint's story was very popular by Catherine's day as religious painting immortalized the content of Voragine's legend. Scenes of saints surrounding the Virgin in glory inevitably included her image, and her mystical espousal with Christ was frequently rendered.[35]

Mary Magdalene's story, in the Voragine collection, emphasized the legendary part of her life after the Resurrection when she became "apostle to the apostles." In the company of Martha, Lazarus, and other disciples of Christ she arrived in Marseilles, France where she preached eloquently to the pagans, performed miracles which brought about important conversions, and established Christianity in that area. Magdalene's final years were spent in penance and contemplation in the total solitude of a cave outside the city; no human food sustained her, and angels nourished her with the food of heavenly company until her death was miraculously brought to the attention of the people of Marseilles who buried her in triumph. [36]

Artistic renditions of Catherine's time also favored Mary Magdalene; her presence in Crucifixion scenes confirmed her importance. Depictions of her solitary ascetic life displayed a gaunt woman roughly clothed, frequently in the long hair reminiscent of her drying Christ's feet with her hair, being visited in her cave either by angels or by Christ Himself bringing her the Eucharist. [37] There is a famous woodcarving of Mary Magdalene by Donatello (1386-1466) aptly demonstrating the medieval emphasis on Magdalene's asceticism and penitential lifestyle. [38] Wrapped in her long hair, she is thin and gaunt, hollow-eyed, and skeletal, befitting one who ate no human food.

Each of these saint's lives emphasizes a woman preaching and teaching with skill and wisdom; each of the legends is preoccupied with food, in both cases sustenance by heavenly food rather than by human nourishment. [39] In Catherine of Alexandria, martyrdom and shedding one's blood lead to eternal life, [40] while in Mary Magdalene, it is solitary prayer and penance which crowns her effort to reach unity with the divine. [41]

Given a formation emphasizing such perceptions of sanctity, Catherine was also influenced by a spirituality relentless in its demand for penance and contrition. In 1354, when Catherine was about seven years of age and struggling with the decision to lead a virginal secluded life, another great Dominican writer and preacher visited Siena, the Florentine Jacopo Passavanti (c. 1300-1357). He achieved fame by his exhortations to penitents as perpetual sinners in the shadow of death and judgment, accompanied by graphic details of the sufferings of the damned in hell. [42] Passavanti represented the tenor of post-plague society. [43]

A young child with a strong desire to be holy, hearing calls for rigorous penance from her preachers, might well entice her playmates to games of whipping with cords and assume a pious demeanor in the presence of adults to impress them with her chosen lifestyle. Moved, on the one hand by the tortured descriptions of Passavanti when he preached from the San Domenico pulpit, and on the other by the emotional piety of Cavalca and Voragine, the youthful Catherine would have difficulty determining her own way. Eventually, she rejected the Florentine self-denial, rationality, and intellectual speculation represented by Passavanti. Influenced by the character of her own civic temperament, she reverted to the Sienese self-abandon, sentiment, and emotion which would lead to the loving relationship of mysticism. [44]

What is admirable is that this child grew to such mature wisdom in the spiritual life that her mystical attending to the Spirit led her to substantial truth, justifying her designation as Doctor of the Church. Her early Dominican training and the role of Tommaso dalle Fonte, Bartolomeo Dominici, and Raymond of Capua become more significant with this insight into her religious formation. Their guiding Catherine through the intricacies of theological expression in her search for a mature spirituality affirms the wisdom of the medieval practice of assigning a theologian to a recognized holy but uneducated woman for her own protection as well as for the preservation of Church teaching.

Ideals of Good Government

Of equal importance in Catherine's intellectual formation were the concepts of justice and the common good which formed the framework of medieval political thought. These principles guided her personal attitude toward the challenging political situations in which she eventually played an active role. Within the walls of the Sienese city hall, the Palazzo Pubblico, are two paintings significant as expressions of the essence of the in-

AMBROSIUS LAURENTIU DE SENIS HIC PINXIT VTRINQVE

21330 - SIENA - Il trionfo della Pace - A. Lorenzetti - Palazzo Pubblico

Anderson Roma

tegrated Sienese civic ideal which nurtured the development of Saint Catherine. One, Ambrogio Lorenzetti's "Allegory of Good Government," secular in subject matter, conveys the religious ideals and principles which should govern rulers. The other, the *"Maestà"* of Simone Martini, is religious in theme, but imparts civic and political ideals directed to the governed.

The first painting, one of a cycle of three frescoes depicting good and bad government, decorates the Salla dalla Pace, the original meeting room of the Nine. Particularly significant since it appeared in 1338-1340, just prior to Catherine's birth into a family steeped in political awareness, Lorenzetti's "Allegory" is a masterful distillation of Aristotelian, Augustinian, and Thomistic teachings; these philosophical, theological, social, and political concepts of government were commonly held or studiously propagated by all active citizens of his time and place. [45] With an inscription in the lower border below the painting, Lorenzetti indicates the two themes which he will elaborate:

> Wherever this holy virtue — Justice — rules, she leads many souls to unity, and these, so united make up the Common Good. . . . [46]

The painting conveys three separate messages: the desirable character of the ruler, Common Good; the significance of Justice and Concord in good government, and the role of citizens in a well-governed commune. Two upper scenes joined by the dominant figure of Peace portray the first two, while a lower portion running the whole length of the fresco illustrates the third.

The section depicting governance portrays a male ruler, Common Good, sitting in a throne. Identified as Sienese by his robe, in the black and white colors of the commune, the ruler holds in his left hand the official shield of the city. Letters above his head, C.S.C.V., establish the locale as "the Commune of Siena, City of the Virgin." Surrounding Common Good, arranged

along an extended sofa-like seat, sit feminine figures representing the virtues and qualities necessary for the administration and
protection of Common Good. On the ruler's right sit Prudence
and Fortitude while set apart to the side is Peace, dressed in
white. To the ruler's left sit Magnanimity, Temperance, and
Justice, while over his head, images of the theological virtues of
Faith, Hope, and Charity depict the motivation of a good Christian
ruler.[47]

To the left of Peace the second scene teaches about the
central ingredient of good government, Justice. The female figure
of Justice is surmounted by Wisdom (also female) and the inscription, "Love Justice, you who rule the earth."[48] Justice holds in
balance the scales of distributive and commutative justice, while
below sits Concord, holding in her left hand two cords which fall
from the two scales. Concord also holds a large carpenter's plane,
symbolizing the equality of citizens in a well regulated society.

Below these scenes, in a long lower portion running the full
length of the fresco, the third message is illustrated by twenty-
four identifiable Sienese citizens who carry the cords of civic unity
which flow from Justice through the hands of Concord. Extending
these cords up to the ruler, Common Good, the citizens demonstrate that the common good is preserved by the harmony, or
Concord, that is preserved by just decisions.[49] From the opposite
side come soldiers guarding prisoners and kneeling knights who
present their castles to Common Good to demonstrate the political fruits of good government described in the rest of the inscription below the allegory:

> Common Good, in order to govern his state, chooses never
> to keep his eyes turned from the splendor of the faces of the
> virtues which around him stand. For this, with triumph are
> given to him taxes, tributes, and lordships of lands; for this,
> without wars is followed then by every civil result, useful,
> necessary, and pleasurable.[50]

The four prominent figures in the overall upper composition —
Common Good, Justice, Concord, and Peace — represent the
important elements of political theory in the Italian communes;
the last two are always dependent upon and result from the
exercise of Justice for the Common Good.[51] This applied not only
to the ruling class but also to all Sienese citizens.

The two subordinate paintings in the cycle reinforce the
importance of the central allegory. On one wall the narrative
portion of the series indicates the effects of good government in
Siena. With an abundance of naturalistic detail, characteristic
both of Lorenzetti and of the early fourteenth century Sienese
school of painting, this fresco conveys a wonderful historic image
of Siena rich with illustrations of life in the city and in the
countryside.[52] The evident tenor of happiness, well being, and
prosperity depicts Siena as a well governed commune.

On the opposite wall is the contrast to this happy scene, a
painting combining both an allegory and a narrative indicating the
effects of bad government. Tyranny presides, surrounded by
figures representing Cruelty, Perfidy, Fraud, Anger, Discord,
and War. The allegory depicts Avarice, Pride, and Vainglory[53] as
the motivation behind the rule of Tyranny, at whose feet sits the
figure of Justice in chains. Fear dominates the citizens as the
narrative portions depict how poorly citizens fare in a town that
lacks good government.

Taken together, the cycle of paintings demonstrated common beliefs as well as creating a "communal secularized
culture." Within weeks of their completion, "every Sienese
writer, poet, and priest, indeed simply every Sienese had seen
them,"[54] so that in the shared existence of late medieval urban
society, they were very likely the focus of heated discussion and
a source of wondrous communal excitement. A century later,
when the famed Franciscan preacher Saint Bernardine of Siena
spoke to throngs assembled in the Campo, he could refer in
detail to the Lorenzetti frescoes with certain expectation that

his hearers would know and understand his references.

Catherine's writings repeatedly express her conception of Justice and the Common Good as central to Peace and Concord. For example, in a letter addressed to the rulers of Bologna, she told them that living in the fear of God would preserve their state and city in peace; that they would safeguard holy justice by rendering what was due to every subject; that they should heed the common good, and not any private good; that they should appoint officials to rule the city, not by party or prejudice, not for flattery or bribery, but with virtue and reason alone. In this way, she stated, their city would be preserved in peace and unity.[55]

Catherine's communications with Pope Gregory XI two decades after the Lorenzetti paintings appeared indicated that her ideas and directives emanated from the understanding of justice and peace held by her society as demonstrated in the paintings.[56] She repeatedly emphasized that peace followed upon justice laced with mercy, never from war or violence; however, justice necessitated the punishment of the wicked. Not to do so would be weakness inviting the prevalence of evil. She wrote:

> Make what terms you can with all your wicked children who have rebelled against you — as far as possible without war, but not without punishing them, as every father must punish the son who offends him.[57]

The second painting, the *"Maestà,"* or the Virgin enthroned in majesty surrounded by saints and angels, contained a corollary teaching about Sienese government. Commissioned in 1315 from Simone Martini for the great Council chamber of the Palazzo Pubblico, its presence there was overtly didactic. Exceeding a purely decorative religious function, the Virgin directly portrayed good citizenship in her role as spiritual ruler and active participant in the decisions of the Council.[58] Justice and the Common Good, ideals in the Lorenzetti fresco directed to the ruling Nine, appear in this *"Maestà"* to encourage citizens to subordinate their individual needs to the Common Good.[59]

The Virgin, the queen and protector of Siena, says through a painted inscription, "But if the powerful molest the weak, your prayers are not for these, nor for anything that deceives my land,"[60] while an inscription on the steps leading to her throne warns against individuals who would disrupt the Common Good:

> The angelic flowers of roses and lilies with which the heavenly field is adorned do not delight me more than good counsel. But sometimes I see one who, for his own advantage, despises me and deceives my lands. . . . Let each one watch for him whom this statement condemns.[61]

The centrality of the Virgin, perhaps even the predominant feminine character of the figures of the Allegory, may have contributed to Catherine's self-confidence as a woman in a medieval society relatively closed to female independence. The unity of medieval life that the paintings conveyed, the integration of religious and civic devotion, would not be lost on Catherine who intuitively accepted the fusion of an active public life and a solitary prayerful one. Duties of citizenship, accepted as a religious responsibility totally relevant to her spiritual life, drew her to the pursuit of peace for the cities of Italy and the purification and reform of the clergy, Papacy, and Church as a pragmatic extension of her own unified interior life.

ENDNOTES

1. William Zinsser, ed., *Extraordinary Lives: Art and Craft of American Biography*, Houghton-Mifflin, Boston, 1986, p. 16.
2. See Daniel J. Levinson, "A Concept of Adult Development," *American Psychologist*, XXXXI (January, 1986), pp. 6-7.
3. Lauro Martines, *Power and Imagination: City-States in Renaissance Italy*, Random House, New York, 1980, pp. 74-75.
4. Ibid., p. 74.

5. The *Noveschi*, Nine Governors and Defenders of the Commune of the People of Siena, were an oligarchy comprised of three representatives of each of the three *terzi* (quarters) of the city who governed Siena from 1287-1355.

6. Statutes of 1287, 1290, and 1310 indicate that Sienese were among the first medievals to engage in city planning to achieve organization and uniformity. See Edna Southard, *The Frescoes in Siena's Palazzo Pubblico, 1289-1539,* Garland Publishing Inc., New York, 1979, p. 10.

7. See Helene Wieruszowski, "Art and the Commune in the Time of Dante," *Speculum,* XIX (1944), p. 15. "The whole conception of public welfare, life, and utility was expressed in this secular architecture. . . . The assemblage of impressive walls and towers in these towns, their gates, fountains, and water reservoirs, their enormous town halls, splendid piazzas for public festivals, loggias for ceremonies, hospitals and churches, reveal even today as the basis of their existence that spirit of municipal community which subordinated the strength and the means of the individual to the purposes of the whole."

8. William Bowsky, *A Medieval Commune: Siena Under the Nine, 1287-1355,* University of California, Berkeley, 1981, p. 19.

9. Tony Hiss, "Experiencing Places, II," *The New Yorker,* June 29, 1987, pp. 76-78.

10. Judith Hook, *Siena: A City and Its History,* Hamish Hamilton, London, 1979, p. 78.

11. Festival space and a building to focus political power and unity was essential to the medieval conception of communal unity. "The communes devoted all their means to stimulating individual endeavor in free competition, and released vigorous forces which until then had been bound by ecclesiastical tradition and religious forms. But they nevertheless imposed new bonds and attached the cultural activity of the citizen to municipal political needs as they had already attached the more material fields of economic life." Wieruszowski, p. 15.

12. This name, popularly applied to the communal tower, referred to the original citizen appointed as bell-ringer in 1347, one known in the town as *mangia,* an idler and consumer of grain.

13. Donald Weinstein and Rudolph Bell, *Saints and Society,* University of Chicago Press, Chicago, 1982, pp. 18, 37.

14. *I, Catherine,* Letter 25, pp. 128-129.

15. Paintings by A. Franchi, expressive of these incidents described in the *Legenda,* have adorned the walls of the kitchen of the former Benincasa residence since 1900.

16. *I, Catherine,* Letter 4, p. 60.

17. Weinstein and Bell, p. 18.

18. Ibid., p. 45.

19. Giacinto D'Urso, O.P., "Il Pensiero di S. Caterina e le sue Fonti," *Sapienza,* VII (1954), p. 377-378. Letters to Bartolomeo Dominici from pre-1374 indicate that he was in nearby Asciano probably preaching a Lenten series. Later that year Catherine wrote to him in Pisa where he was in residence at the Dominican house of studies there. *Letters,* 4-6, 8-9, 20-21, pp. 45-84.

20. D'Urso, ibid., pp. 335-388.

21. Ibid., p. 377.

22. In the *Legenda,* Raymond stated, "Wishing to emulate Blessed Dominic who had appeared to her she disciplined herself with an iron chain three times a day. . . . In the story of St. Dominic's life it says that the famous Father usually did this, and for a long time she did the same." (L. 55) Paintings by Fra Angelico in the friars' cells in the monastery of San Marco in Florence indicate some of these elements of Dominican

teaching and practice; there is especial emphasis on Christ's blood — Dominic is shown washed in the blood flowing from his side; friars freely use the discipline, drawing blood in the process; both the Virgin Mary and Mary Magdalene appear with great frequency.

23. Thomas J. Johnston, O.P., "Franciscan and Dominican Influences on the Medieval Order of Penance: Origins of the Dominican Laity," *Spirituality Today*, 37 (Summer, 1985), pp. 115-117.

24. D'Urso, p. 379.

25. Pope Gregory the Great (c. 540-604; reigned 590-604) was a prolific writer; his *Dialogues* — conversations with Peter the Deacon about sixth century saints — were equal in importance to Augustine's *City of God* of an earlier period, earning him the distinction of being the finest exponent of the Christian way of life in the middle ages. As noted previously, Catherine always adapted and expanded the symbols of her day; Noffke likens her delineation of the "Bridge" in her *Dialogue* to the Ponte Vecchio, the famous bridge spanning the Arno in Florence which was complete with shops and places of refreshment; her "tree of virtue" resembled a tree of nature in full bloom.

26. Ubertino of Casale (c. 1259-1329-41) wrote of the life and passion of Christ in his *Arbor vitae crucifixae Jesu* (1304-1305); this work also included ecstatic meditations on Saint Francis, on poverty, and harsh criticisms of the laxity of the upper clergy.

27. Two hundred thirty-three manuscript copies of this work (c. 400-416) date from the ninth through the fifteenth century, testifying to its popularity in the later middle ages. *The Trinity*, in *The Fathers of the Church*, v. 45, tr. by Stephen McKenna, C.SS.R., Catholic University of America Press, 1963, vii, xi.

28. D'Urso, pp. 365-367.

29. See Kenelm Foster, O.P., "Vernacular Scriptures in Italy," in *The Cambridge History of the Bible*, Vol. II, ed. by G.W.H. Lampe, the University Press, Cambridge, 1969, pp. 452-465.

30. The question of Catherine's ability to read is an interesting one since Raymond indicated that she learned the skill "miraculously." (L. 96-97) Medieval comments on abilities to read and write were based on a high professional standard, perhaps that of the notary, of the educated teacher, or the privileged upper class person. The highly touted Hildegard of Bingen, always referred to as uneducated, dictated all her work, even her famous illuminations, detail by detail, to a personal scribe. Probably Catherine could read in a very rudimentary fashion; since frequently mothers were responsible for this training in their daughters, Catherine's dependence on Lapa for assistance would not predicate much success. The miraculous ability to read was more than likely a personal effort undertaken after intense prayer, to learn to read the divine office with the help of her followers. The ability to write, always minimal, was achieved in a similar manner during her enforced isolation at Rocca d'Orcia in the fall of 1377.

31. Francesco de Sanctis, *History of Italian Literature*, tr. by Joan Redfern, Harcourt, Brace, New York, 1931, 2V., I, p. 121.

32. Commenting on the virtue of obedience in the *Dialogue*, Catherine wrote, "The person you read about in *The Lives of the Fathers*. . . ." and "You will recall having read it in *The Lives of the Fathers*." The examples she cited were the disciple who continued to water a dry stick day after day in obedience to his superior, and another who stopped his writing in the middle of a letter out of obedience, to find it completed in gold on his return. (D. 164:357-358)

33. *The Golden Legend of Jacobus de Voragine*, tr. by Granger Ryan and Helmut Ripperger, Longmans, Green and Co., New York, 2nd printing, 1948, Foreword, pp. v-xiii.

34. Voragine, p. 708-716. For an image of Catherine being tortured on a spiked wheel, see Guido da Siena's "Reliquary Shutters," (1255-1260) in *The World of Giotto, c. 1267-1337*, Sarel Eimerl & eds. of *Time-Life Books*, Time, Inc., New York, 1967, p. 74. One can speculate on the influence of the details of this legend on Raymond as he endeavored to assure the canonization of Catherine of Siena by emphasizing likenesses with known saints; in the legend there is an account of Catherine of Alexandria's finger breaking off spontaneously in response to a petitioner's prayer for a relic; after Catherine of Siena's death in Rome, Raymond directed the removal of Catherine's head and finger and their return to Siena where they are kept as relics to this day.

35. See Millard Meiss, *Painting in Florence and Siena after the Black Death*, Princeton University Press, New Jersey, 1978 ed., figs. 100, 105-107. An informal check during a retrospective of the paintings from Catherine's day in the Pinacoteca National Gallery in Siena showed that despite the frequency of Crucifixion scenes, which almost always included Mary Magdalene, Catherine of Alexandria was a more popular representation than Magdalene who was a close second among females; women saints were a consistent presence in medieval altar panels which arrayed four to six saints around the primary subject.

36. Voragine, pp. 355-364. Raymond also emphasized the significance of Magdalene; his interpretation of Catherine's total reliance on the Eucharist as food was probably patterned on Voragine's legend.

37. All of these scenes are depicted in the "St. Mary Magdalene Altarpiece," from the second half of the 13th century; see Eimerl, *Giotto*, p. 23. Catherine's reception of Holy Communion was frequently facilitated by Christ, either directly or through divine inspiration of a reluctant cleric; see, for example, D. 142:294; 111:210-211; 142:294-295.

38. La Maddalena (c. 1453-55), Opera del Duomo, Florence; Donatello has a similar woodcarving of John the Baptist, perhaps emphasizing the likeness of her penitential lifestyle to that of the Baptist. Fillipo Lippi also pictured Magdalene in this fashion with John the Baptist (c. 1457), Academia, Florence. Interestingly enough, none of the painted renditions of Catherine of Siena coming from her contemporaries portray her as emaciated or reveal any effects of malnourishment.

39. The question of medieval abstinence from food has a contemporary fascination in connection with the present day interest in anorexia; however, it was common practice for holy women in medieval society to deny themselves food. The very repetition of this type of abnegation pointed more directly to definitions of sanctity peculiar to the medieval world, than to a recurring illness of one particular nature in all or any of these women. See Rudolph Bell, *Holy Anorexia*, University of Chicago Press, Chicago, 1985, for an interpretation of the fasting practices of medieval holy women. Though his concept of a "holy" anoretic is interesting, Bell appears to use hagiographical "facts" in place of empirical data. In addition, he fails to integrate concepts of medieval symbolism; for example, in the area of breast feeding, so significant to his interpretation, he fails to move beyond the narrow mother/daughter aspect to the broader symbolic meaning of this very prevalent medieval artistic symbolic device. Renditions of the act of nursing abounded in the medieval world, concretizing a conception of nourishing relationships. Portrayals of the Virgin nursing her child had deep connotational meaning to individuals; the Church was presented as

a woman suckling infants at both breasts, symbolizing the spiritual nourishment dispensed through this institution. See also Caroline Bynum, *Holy Feast and Holy Fast*, University of California Press, Berkeley, 1986; her interpretation of "the religious significance of food to medieval women" is a feasible one.

40. In a letter to Raymond, Catherine described her aborted opportunity for martyrdom in the violence and tumult of Florence, where she was residing in 1377-78 as papal emissary. Her disappointment was great, but we learn something of her concept of the value of martyrdom from her reaction. She wrote, "but my desire to give my life for the Truth and the sweet Bride of Christ was not fulfilled. . . . So I have reason to weep . . . , that I did not deserve that my blood should give life, or illumine darkened minds, or reconcile the sons with the father, or cement a stone in the mystical body of Holy Church." Scudder, p. 258.

41. It was in the *Legenda*, not in the *Dialogue*, that overt references were made to the similarities between Catherine's life and incidents in the lives of these very well known saints.

42. de Sanctis, pp. 123-124.

43. John Larner, *Culture and Society in Italy, 1290-1420*, Charles Scribner's Sons, London, 1971, pp. 130-132; see also Meiss, chap. 3, for an examination of the guilt, penance, and rapture which followed on the plague epidemic.

44. Meiss, p. 85; Larner, *Culture and Society*, p. 132.

45. See Nicolai Rubinstein, "Political Ideals in Sienese Art: The Frescoes by Ambrogio Lorenzetti and Taddeo di Bartolo in the Palazzo Pubblico," *Journal of the Warburg and Courtauld Institutes, XXI* (1958) for a detailed development of the ingredients of medieval concepts of justice, peace, and wisdom in the Aristotelian, Augustinian, and Thomist traditions; Rubinstein advances the theory that Lorenzetti, though philosophically inclined, was not the author of the concept of the allegory. He stated, "it is more likely that some learned notary or chancellor with legal training and philosophical interests was the author . . ." p. 182 ff. Allegorical figures in secular art were based primarily on the symbolic language developed for the decorative art of the churches, but integrated with symbols and images drawn from pagan legends, mythology, and classical allusions. Wieruszowski, pp. 24, 27.

46. Hook, p. 84. Giotto initiated this medieval tradition of interpreting the political realities of his day by means of allegorical paintings; he was the first to introduce the allegory of the commune and the nature of the government it provided; however, Lorenzetti was the first to illustrate the ruler as "Common Good" and government by citizens rather than by a powerful lord or Bishop. Wieruszowski, pp. 23-25; see also Rubinstein, pp. 180-182.

47. Conventional medieval political theory had emphasized that a ruling prince should observe the cardinal virtues and additional "political" virtues deemed essential; here, Lorenzetti pictured the four cardinal virtues, adding Magnanimity and Peace. Rubinstein, p. 180.

48. The connection between wisdom and justice was expounded in Thomas Aquinas' treatise on law; civil lawyers propounded that justice should be inspired by reason; but, wisdom as the guiding principle of good government was part of a long standing medieval tradition based on Roman and Biblical precedents. Rubinstein, p. 183.

49. The cords were carried by known personages of the town, who, facing toward Common Good, demonstrated that justice was the guiding principle of the common good. In Catherine's time, the Italian city-republics believed they had discovered an alternative to despotic rule in the concept of the superiority of common good to

individual welfare: "In the early fourteenth century, it becomes a commonplace in political and didactic prose and poetry that only by placing common welfare above private interest can internal peace, economic prosperity and political power be secured and preserved; so does the view that neglect of the common good leads to civic strife and the decline and fall of cities." Rubinstein, p. 184.

50. Bowsky, p. 289.
51. In medieval political theory, peace and concord represented the most desirable effects of just government in the interests of the common good, derived from Thomist, Augustinian, and Roman thought. Rubinstein, p. 187.
52. Commenting on the significance of the new interest in naturalism and the portrayal of real people in this type of medieval painting, Wieruszowski stated, "Didactic and political subjects required an especially clear and distinct language in order that the lessons taught should be fully understood by the citizens. The task demanded qualities of observation and imitation; allegory was to be placed in the natural environment of the observer, and hence the depicting of the city with its characteristic architectural features and representative buildings." p. 29
53. This is a powerful example of painting providing insight into the classical-medieval mind; here, the vices most feared because they seemed to threaten the harmony of their new political world were castigated, like the three beasts of the *Divine Comedy*, avarice, pride, and vainglory.
54. Meiss, p. 131.
55. Scudder, pp. 208-209.
56. See below, Part Three, for a development of this theme.
57. *I, Catherine*, Letter 23, p. 124. In this she demonstrated the contemporary understanding that punishable crimes were violations of justice. Rubinstein, pp. 182-183.
58. Wieruszowski stated, "There, as queen of the city, she might personally assist at the council meetings and inspire the authorities to wise decisions." p. 19.
59. See Rubinstein, p. 179.
60. Bowsky, p. 286.
61. Ibid.

2

THE CHURCH:
PAPACY, CLERGY, AND FAITHFUL

In the fourteenth century of Saint Catherine of Siena, the Christian Church dominated the external political world even as it regulated the personal and spiritual life of every individual. [1] Not only religious practice, but every event of significance revolved around the Church. In addition, the world of Catherine was a world in constant flux, one which reacted to repeated war, pestilence, and hunger at the same time that innovative commercial enterprise initiated new political and social institutions. In Italy, the growth of urban populations had resulted in communes and city-states like Catherine's native Siena, while in other areas of western Europe a rapidly expanding monarchial tradition encouraged the development of a sense of national and ethnic singularity. Each of these tendencies was destined to confront and disrupt radically the unity of medieval Christendom which had permitted the dominance of papal power in political as well as religious matters.

Underlying the religious ferment, both institutional and personal, was the influence of the Gregorian reform movement initiated by Pope Gregory VII (1073-1085). This Benedictine monk, Hildebrand, was eager to instill in the Church at large the instincts of the Benedictine monastic reform movement of the previous century. His political confrontation with the Holy Roman Empire, designed to limit monarchial control over local Church prelates, accelerated the growth of papal power over secular rulers. However, Gregory's program embraced a far broader and deeper internal renewal: the reform of the total Church, clerical and lay. Central to his transforming purpose was the revision of clerical life. His call for a return to the personal holiness of the apostolic life as lived by Christ and the Apostles included a mandate for clerical celibacy as well as an end to venal practices which had crept into Church routine.

The currents of such attempts to reform influenced several issues which were to increase in importance during the later middle ages. Redefinition of clerical life began to alter the traditional Augustinian concept of the Church as one body of the faithful, inclusive of both laity and clergy. Gradually, the Church began to demonstrate an authoritarian consciousness of clerical distinction and to press for conformity and discipline in its subjects. Clerical celibacy and monastic reform altered traditional monastic roles for women. Those women who had been educated and allowed participation in quasi-clerical functions were soon forced to seek new ways to serve God and the Church. At the same time, the urban laity began to demand clearer teaching and a more vibrant spirituality as their new economic and political status caused increased personal conflicts. Finally, and most significant for Church history, the temporal power of the Papacy, initiated and rapidly expanded under Gregory VII, peaked and then faltered as the middle ages drew to a close.

Since this was the world which eventually drew Catherine to action, she must be seen against its background for she was formed by its customs and activities, by the spirituality which it fostered, and by its conception of God and relationship with the Divine.

The Papacy

By the time of the reign of Innocent III (1198-1216) Gregory VII's assertion of papal authority over secular rulers had become a reality. Pope Innocent, as the sole effective international arbiter, displayed authority sufficient to enforce papal decisions. Yet, as with all power, his domination contained within it the destructive seeds of decay; reaching a pinnacle, his flagrant authoritarianism set in motion the decline of the temporal dominance of the papacy. Consequently, during the next century, when Boniface VIII (1294-1303) attempted to hold firm to the traditional papal prerogative of political supremacy with its freedom to intervene in the internal affairs of any state, he failed in the contest for papal preeminence over the new national spirit represented by the French monarch, King Philip IV, the Fair.

In 1303, under duress to obey a papal injunction against taxation of the clergy, Philip demonstrated the power and solidarity of the new national spirit when he sent troops to attack Pope Boniface VIII at his summer residence in the Italian hill town of Agnani. Boniface was captured and harassed before being released by the efforts of the townspeople.[2] This pivotal event heralded a significant change in relationships which was dramatically demonstrated by the failure of traditionally effective papal sanctions such as excommunication and interdict.[3] Applied as punishments to the French King, they failed to weaken Philip's control either over his lay subjects or over the French clergy.

Six years later, in 1309, the French Archbishop who became Clement V (1305-1314), moved the papal court from Rome and took up residence in Avignon, an independent papal territory on the Rhône River. The Avignon Papacy, significantly influenced by succeeding French Popes, French Cardinals, and a Gallic way of life began to lose its authenticity as an impartial international mediator, further weakening the political dominance of the Church of Rome.

However, the Avignon Papacy developed a well organized and effective government center, attending efficiently to judicial, financial, and legislative concerns. If its character was less spiritual than in previous times, it was in keeping with that of secular governments. Confronted with dramatic increases in administrative duties and functions, both governments required additional personnel to deal with the expanding concerns of effective political leadership and financial stability. The papal court also followed secular governments in its adoption of worldly tastes and manners. With its affectation of the splendor of secular court life in dress, food, and entertainment, the papacy appeared less and less to reflect its primary reason for existence, the moral and spiritual leadership of all Christendom, at the very time that a new urban spirituality was demanding a heightened sense of the value of Gospel poverty.

The founding and flourishing of the new mendicant orders, the Franciscans and the Dominicans, correlated well with urbanization and its demand for simplicity of life. These religious groups, espousing corporate as well as personal poverty, voluntarily renounced endowments of land and wealth as well as the enclosure of the older monastic traditions. Instead, they chose to depend on charity and almsgiving for all the necessities of life and to involve themselves actively in the lives of townspeople.

Francis of Assisi (c. 1182-1226) espoused poverty in direct imitation of the poverty of Jesus Christ whom he desired to emulate in all things. The thousands from all over western Europe who came to follow the Franciscan way of life testified to the wide appeal of this radical attitude in his time and place; however, this outcome was somewhat trying to the saint for whom the idea and leadership of an international organization became an unintended responsibility.

In contrast, Dominic (1170-1221) deliberately set out to establish an order, organized in primitive simplicity based on the Augustinian rule and tradition of public service, but primarily concerned with an apostolate of combating heresy and defending Christian truth through preaching. From its inception, the Dominican Order made preaching its primary work; consequently, education, university training, and scholarship received special emphasis. [4] Saint Thomas Aquinas, the famous thirteenth century Dominican, taught that the highest life was that in which the fruits of contemplation were shared with others in an active life. Such a concept was actually an intellectual extension of the original conception of Dominic.

At the same time, there flourished in urban areas all over southern Europe a highly emotional lay piety accompanied by a headstrong independence. In some cases, such fervor began to display an increasingly critical attitude toward the clergy and the practices of the Church. Beginning with opposition to ecclesiastical pomp and wealth, this friction quickly extended into the political arena; it gradually encompassed dogmatic and sacramental questions; finally, it questioned Church authority. These were challenges to which the Church could not remain indifferent.

Heresy and fear of heresy became a more frequent preoccupation in the life of the Church from the closing years of the twelfth century onward. Because divisiveness had more than doctrinal implications — it was a threat to the unity of all Christendom — the attitude of the papacy stiffened toward popular movements of lay piety and penitence among Christians. A climate of divisive hostility continued into the fourteenth century when the papacy began to articulate a conservatism which distanced it and sometimes placed it in opposition to the new intellectual currents of the times. A fear, bordering on repression, was demonstrated not only in hostility to popular urban religious movements, but also in the silencing of spiritual thinkers like William of Ockham, Marsilius of Padua, and Meister Eckhart of the Rhineland. This attitude extended to condemnations, for example, of the Franciscan doctrine of poverty in 1323. However, the new ferment was too strong to be repressed. Articulate lay opinion about religion, disseminated from the towns, stimulated new ideas and new movements which remained integral to the religious life of the later middle ages. [5]

In Catherine's day, the Avignon residence of the Pope was a

major concern in Italian politics since the quality of administration in the papal territories in Italy was poor. Appointed leaders, both lay and religious, seemed more interested in their own profit than in the administration of justice and the welfare of their subjects. Catherine became involved when she endeavored to diminish tensions between these Italian city-states and the papacy and to restore order and social harmony in the papal territories. Drawn into papal politics as intercessor for the Florentine Republic, she went to Avignon to the court of Pope Gregory XI (1370-1378) in the pursuit of peace. Her public role intensified when, addressing the crisis of papal authority, she became a compassionate critic of the morality and politics of the fourteenth century Church. She joined her voice to those who urged the return of the papal court to Rome as she advocated spiritual and administrative reform.

Catherine's influence with Gregory was one of the motivating factors behind his returning the papal court to Rome in 1376 after its location in Avignon for almost seventy years. What seemed like a final resolution of this long standing problem led to further complications at Gregory's death the following year when an Italian, Urban VI, was elected Pope. Reformist in tendency and irascible in temperament, Urban soon alienated many Cardinals who, asserting that he had been selected under pressure from Roman officials, denied the validity of his election, withdrew, and elected a French Cardinal as Pope. The simultaneous reign of a Pope in Rome and in Avignon, known as the Great Schism, further splintered a Church already straining for unity. Catherine's final years were devoted to seeking a resolution of this schism. Summoned to Rome, she spent her failing energies in mustering political, military, and spiritual support for the Urbanist cause.

These dramatic changes in the spiritual and political nature of the papacy, as well as the continuance of unsettling political conditions both in the papal temporal domain and throughout Italy, were of concern to Catherine throughout her life. Petitioning, preaching, and praying, she spent herself for the reform of the "mystic body of Holy Church" and for the return of peace and harmony to the Christian world.

Urban Piety

The growth of an urban society radically altered the life concepts of fourteenth century people. Friction between newly emerging social patterns and older traditions, apparent at every level of society, required adjustments not only in social, political, intellectual, and cultural areas but also in religious life and practice. A rudimentarily educated clergy, once satisfactory to the needs of a rural population, no longer sufficed. Neither did a liturgical and spiritual system geared to the agricultural seasons and the life and death eventualities of the poor and unlettered peasant masses. City dwellers demanded a clergy educated to meet their growing intellectual and cultural standards. At the same time, they were attracted to the spirit of poverty and simplicity professed in the Gospel message of Jesus Christ, the spirit promulgated by the Gregorian reform. Contrasts between ostentatious urban wealth and ideals of religious poverty, between the old traditions of ritual practice and a new need for highly emotional expressions of pious ardent faith, underlay the heightened sensitivities of townspeople in prosperous commercial centers.

Cities like Siena were microcosms of the new urban society in which citizens, newly rich from enlarged opportunities in lucrative overland trade and commerce, were increasingly self-confident and independent; ferment grew from their self-consciousness about maintaining religious fervor in the midst of new conditions. An intensity, ardor, and dynamism, previously unknown among the rural peasantry or the landed aristocracy of the countryside, characterized the religious expression of urban people. The motivation behind the building of cathedrals, hospitals, and universities in medieval cities and towns, this vibrant faith sometimes led its enthusiasts into confrontation with the institutional Christian Church, itself caught up in the extravagances newly available with the influx of luxury items into the trade centers of western Europe.

Generally dissatisfied with the parish clergy of the towns, lay persons looked to the mendicant friars — Franciscans and Dominicans — for models of devotional life. Thus, urban lay piety of this period began to resemble monastic spirituality with its stress on the evangelical counsels of poverty, chastity, obedience and a well developed interior formation. [6] It is not unrelated that during this period the sacramental system of the Church became a more established and intimate part of the daily life of Christians. [7] Baptism, Confirmation, Matrimony, and even Extreme Unction were given additional liturgical expression; the reception of the Eucharist became a more regular option for the laity, making communion with God an experienced reality. [8]

Even living out the Gospel by adopting a religious way of life while remaining "in the world" became a distinct possibility for lay persons when the mendicants devised tertiary or third orders. Living in their own homes under rule without embracing the common life, men and women could be active in works of charity and zealous in personal prayer and penance without interrupting their ordinary economic activities. (L. 66-68)[9] Originally, the third orders had attracted married couples; by Catherine's day, these groups persisted primarily in Italy, consisting of widows of mature age who chose not to remarry. Later, following her example, there were more cases of younger single women living as tertiaries. (L. 67-68)

With the advent of more dramatic, enthusiastic, and extreme religious tendencies, new religious groups began to flourish in urban areas throughout Europe. These, too, drew male and female members, usually married, who espoused voluntary poverty; frequently, they lived in common, either continuing their ordinary occupations or choosing humble manual labor and/or begging. [10] It is neither possible nor necessary to examine each one of these movements; however, it is generally clear that none of them were founded as alternatives to the established Church. Renewal and conversion of life were the underlying and motivating factors in every case.

Friction frequently occurred, however, since the impulse of the Gregorian Reform gave a heightened significance to clerical status at the same time that the laity sought new freedom to express their relationship to God. The practice of one group, the *Humiliati*, to preach and teach publicly, was initially condemned (1184). Later, Innocent III approved of lay preaching, distinguishing between the clerical prerogative to teach doctrine and lay preaching to give witness in matters of faith and morals. [11] This distinction would have a direct bearing on Catherine's being permitted to preach and teach in her day.

Church authority, operating to elevate the role of priest, caused a growing separation between clergy and the faithful, thereby widening the breach between the laity and the hierarchy. Though these differences have been characterized as quarrels within a united family, since individuals believed that they were firmly orthodox, the danger inherent in the localism and independence of the lay impulses — resistance to control and responsibility — raised a problem that the Church attempted to counteract by the imposition of ordered hierarchical authority. [12]

While the laity began to feel estranged from a hierarchy which demanded conformity, the growth of the medieval cult of the Virgin mediated a direct relationship with the Deity. Modeling a more personal spiritual ideal of womanhood, devotion to Mary emphasized qualities of motherhood which illustrated her human nature. Medieval painting is rich with examples demonstrating this new vision of Mary and, consequently, of her Child. In Siena, for example, the intensity of relationship with the Virgin was shown by its devotion to "Madonna Lactans," or "Madonna Del Latte," the nursing mother. The Sienese Ambrogio Lorenzetti was the first artist to paint this warmly human medieval subject on canvas, thereby heightening the intimate, loving, human element of Mary's mothering of her Child. Even more significant was the Sienese popular extension of this motherly devotion to her divine Child into a conception that Mary nursed Siena at her breast. A refrain popular in Catherine's day underlined this intimate though mythical relationship:

> You . . . in order to give your milk to Siena, deprived the
> heavenly child of his share. [13]

This Sienese perception of Mary as the Mother who nursed their city at her own breast exemplifies the intimacy of the association with the Mother of God discerned by the medieval mind.

A corollary to devotion to the Mother was devotion to the divine Child. It was difficult to fear a Child frequently imaged as playing with birds or nursing at his Mother's breast; hence, the emergence of Mary as loving Mother led to a more humanized image of the Deity. [14] Qualities of mercy, charity, and compassion enabled love to enter the human/divine encounter. A warm relationship with divinity produced an interiorized religious devotion not possible with the conception of a judgmental God who provoked fear and awe without a foundation of love.

A personal God, to whom Saint Francis of Assisi could relate with such loving intimacy, emerged not only among the saintly but also as an inspiration to a pious laity. Sanctity, attainable through prayer, personal dedication, imitation, and sacramental grace, no longer was reserved for the erudite; a loving relationship with God was within the reach of the average person. In addition to the pictorial art of the period which amply testified to this changing concept, [15] figurative devotional representations appeared, such as the Child of the manger recalling Christ's nativity; here was the ultimate expression of a God, helpless, human, and approachable.

This incarnate image of God, with its accentuation of the divine experiential sharing in human fragility, was accompanied by, or resulted in, the emergence of a Christianity newly conscious of the Gospel call to care for one's neighbor: the poor, the sick, and the helpless of society. [16] Simultaneously, urban life had diminished the boundaries between classes; persons of great wealth came into intimate contact with the comfortable bourgeois, the poor, the helpless, and the needy in a manner totally different from the pre-commercial, agricultural, rural lifestyle. Feminine nurturing qualities, affirming love and caring charity, reentered the practice of Christianity through the influence of the ideal woman, the Mother of God. Personal love of the neighbor for the love of God, the second great commandment preached by Jesus Christ, resumed its rightful place in Christian teaching.

The strange dichotomy of a laity growing in personal intimacy with God and the Virgin, while estranged from official religious authority, charged the atmosphere. The papacy, already contending for political supremacy with the kings of newly emerging nation states, was forced to defend its authority over powerful lay urban religious groups lest the growth of heretical sects divide the unity of Christendom. These factors operated in a superstructure whose foundation was itself in flux as changing patterns of family life, new civic and national awareness, and emotional strains of pious religious expression made change more constant than custom. In historical periods dominated by multifaceted tensions such as these, periods marked by social displacement in traditional roles and the emergence of new stereotypes, women frequently experience additional freedom to participate in society. [17]

Changes in established gender patterns, newly translated from traditional agricultural settings to the towns, contributed to the overall dynamism of the period. The combination of new roles for women with increased emphasis on gospel traditions caused older modes of accepted activity for holy women to reappear with new vigor. Role models — the companions of Jesus, deaconesses, prophetesses, ascetic hermits, and the early martyrs — incorporated a uniquely feminine dimension of witness and/or service, some characterized by singular forcefulness, power, and even leadership. [18]

Women in the Medieval Church

In the earlier middle ages monastic life for women owed its foundation and support to wealthy widows who retired to monasteries which they generously endowed. [19] Members were upper class women who devoted themselves to intellectual pursuits similar to those of their male counterparts. Double monasteries prevailed until about the twelfth century; in this schema co-equal but separate monastic houses for men and women were governed as one, at times, by an Abbess who functioned with jurisdictional powers equivalent to a bishop. Artistic representations of female monastic superiors, Saint Bridgid of Ireland for example, depict them holding the crosier, symbolic of a feudal Lord's political and legal authority as the ruler of a monastic landed estate.

Recent scholarship has raised our awareness of one of these early monastic leaders, Hildegard of Bingen, a mystic notable for preaching and teaching, for organizing and reforming, for establishing monasteries, for composing, writing, healing, and prophesying. [20] Hildegard's achievement in art, music, and poetry, in nine books on theology, physiology, health, religious biography, and interpretive commentaries was unique and dramatic. The variety and quality of her work, however, suggests the type of activity which engaged these medieval residents of the double monasteries for whom education and opportunity for leadership in the Church was an accepted option, albeit the only one, during this early period. [21]

A definitive change in this climate of opinion ensued as continuing momentum for clerical reform gave rise to new monastic orders in the Church. The Premonstratensians, for example, founded early in the twelfth century, attracted women members in large numbers. Originally open to the sponsorship of female foundations, by 1200 the Order had decreed that no more women could be admitted. [22] A similar procedure marked the Cistercian experience whereby female foundations, enthusiastically adopting the rigorous and austere discipline of the male monasteries, came into being without formal approval, but were also rejected. [23]

Exceptions to this general trend occurred when powerful and/or influential sponsors encouraged clerical support of female foundations or when individual clerics took special interest in the spiritual well-being of groups of nuns; nevertheless, definitive attitudes and new legislation regarding clerical status significantly altered the traditional concept of a female monastery. Consequently, angry exchanges often were the result of this tightened hierarchical control as quasi-clerical functions, long the prerogative of female monastic leaders, were gradually prohibited. These had included blessing, investing with the habit, and mutual confession and forgiveness of sin in the absence of an authorized monk or other Church minister. A critical result of this change in attitude toward women was that the few opportunities for leadership in the Church that had been available to monastic women of the earlier period no longer existed. Parallel to this change and equally significant, the quality of education provided in early monastic settings deteriorated to the point that a body of educated women no longer existed to participate in the intellectual life of the Church.

Though monastic life continued to be a viable option retaining appeal for some women, many of the new urban middle class, inspired by the same zeal and independence as the heretical or fringe movements, were more attracted to new forms. Lay women, participating fully in the emotional pietism of the new religious movements, were more self-directed and desirous to learn from their own experience; hence, they sought new expressions for a committed lay religious life. [24] Newer forms suited the non-clerical, non-institutional, non-cloistered female, one who, living in the world, became a model of a dedicated life attractive to a religious minded laity seeking an example emanating from their own secular lifestyle.

In southern Europe, Italy particularly, the most common expression was the tertiary community attached to the mendicant orders; this option gave Catherine of Siena authenticity in the Church and direction in her spiritual life. Tertiaries lived in their own homes under rule in obedience to superiors; they had a formal prayer life including penance and ascetical practices, the fruit of which was to be manifested in active engagement in charitable work, not unlike the confraternities which had come into being in almost every Italian city.

Alternative expressions of a dedicated religious life arose in northern Europe. In England, recluses or anchoresses were common. A freer more independent form emerged in the Rhineland and Lowlands where groups of women known as Beguines were very numerous. A chronicler in 1250 reported more than a thousand in the environs of Cologne alone. [25] They lived commonly in poverty and chastity with great austerity favoring manual labor, service, and contemplative prayer. Disregarding formal organization, they had neither hierarchy of authority, nor formal rule, nor vows indicating permanent commitment. Though these groups became well known for the quality and holiness of their lives, because of their lack of acceptable organizational forms and official confirmation, they soon came into conflict with the institutional Church, moving steadily in the direction of more, rather than less, authoritarian structures. In 1312 the Council of Vienne issued the following decree:

We have been told that certain women commonly called Beguines, afflicted with a kind of madness, discuss the Holy Trinity and the divine essence, and express opinions on matters of faith and sacraments contrary to the catholic faith, deceiving many simple people. Since these women promise no obedience to anyone and do not denounce their property or profess an approved Rule, they are certainly not "religious," although they wear a habit and are associated with such religious orders as they find congenial. . . . We have therefore decided and decreed with the approval of the Council that their way of life is to be permanently forbidden and altogether excluded from the Church of God. [26]

The severity of this language did not translate into immediate action although eventually many Beguines were forced to join established religious institutions of a more traditional nature. However, when Catherine's biographer, Raymond of Capua, gave a short history of the Sisters of Penance of Saint Dominic in the *Legenda*, he made explicit reference to the plight of the Beguines and distanced the Dominican tertiaries from them:

[W]hen Pope John XXII promulgated his *Clementina* against the *Beghine* [sic] and the *Begardi* [the male equivalent] he stated in another Bull that the decree did not apply to the Sisters of Penance of St. Dominic in Italy and that the value of their state was in no way lessened by it. (L. 68)

Emphasis on rule, obedience, and formal procedure among the Dominican tertiaries more than likely tightened as a result of the controversy over the Beguines, but the Sisters of Penance of Saint Dominic, or Mantellate, had always been under the direct authority of the Church through the Master General of the Dominican Order.

Female Mystics

The characteristic spirituality of many of these lay religious women was mysticism, attractive to town dwellers already emotionally prepared for intense religious experience. Commenting on medieval mysticism, Caroline Bynum stressed the importance of this period in the religious history of women:

> For the first time in Christian history we can document that a particular kind of religious experience is more common among women than men. For the first time in Christian history certain major devotional and theological emphases emanate from women and influence the basic development of spirituality. [27]

Several factors contributed to the significance of mysticism and the prevalence of women as mystics in this time period. Among these, the new emotional content of urban piety and the non-institutional forms of religious expression permitted to holy women were important. Whether living at home or in religious groups, holy women frequently chose a solitary existence so that they could be absorbed in a personal experience of God. Their piety, influenced by the emotional prayer forms of the day, encouraged imaginative meditation before paintings and icons which, influenced by new artistic forms, were laden with naturalistic detail and humanistic subject matter. Direct contact with the holy subjects was explicitly invited. [28] Emphasis on the human Christ and the Virgin Mother encouraged intimacy, as did frequent access to the Eucharist and to the sacramental system. In addition, elaborate stories of holiness, quite popular at this time, contributed to a highly cultivated imagination.

Cut off from options open to holy men — educators, priests, active mendicant friars and brothers, founders and leaders of confraternities for service to the community — the women lived in the midst of the commune, knew intimately the vicissitudes of daily life experienced by their community, and shared in all the local concerns. Though powerless in the social sense to effect change directly or even to determine the course of their own lives independently, they emanated a power, an energy, and an authority more forceful than any conveyed by external office or by social class. Because of their direct experience of God in prayer, holy women were seen as a divine gift to the community, a mediating presence before God for those who struggled to remain above the sinful realities of life or to repent of them. They drew townspeople like a magnet once they came to public attention. As their circles of influence widened, some, like Catherine of Siena, were drawn into the larger religious/political questions of the day.

In many ways the example of Catherine of Siena is typical, even though her prestige surpassed the majority of women of her day. Well known to neighbors from childhood, Catherine's adolescent determination to live a virginal life as a Dominican tertiary was unusual in itself because of her youth and unmarried status. Her years of silence and solitude did not go unnoticed so that when she emerged from seclusion to practice public acts of charity, she became an object of curiosity. Authentication of her singular holiness came first from followers; a "family" began to form almost immediately, composed of friars, prominent citizens, and women, many of whom were Mantellate. Requests for her guidance in spiritual as well as social and political crises tested her; the resulting repentance for sin, conversion of life, restoration of harmonious relationships, or decisions marked by a dedication to peace and justice confirmed the authenticity of her interior power and wisdom. These results brought her to the attention of religious authorities. [29]

Authentication by an official decree of the Dominican Order, repeated in a papal bull of Pope Gregory XI, was the final affirmation of Catherine's status as holy person. The appointment of a confessor, customary for holy women of the time, ensured the inviolability of the teachings of the Church by preserving the distinction of the clerical role. It allowed Catherine to speak for the Church as a model of the virtuous life and to convey to hearts hungry for divine wisdom the fruits of her extraordinary holiness. In this way, she became a mediator between the hierarchical Church and a sometimes disenchanted laity.

An official confessor also protected Catherine. People of her violent age dealt harshly with those who asserted authority and/ or demonstrated unusual powers. The distinction between saint/ witch and mystic/sorceress was a fine one to a society preoccupied with the spirit world. At once attracted to preternatural manifestations, they were yet suspicious of them; punishment of one believed to be allied with the devil and the powers of darkness was swift as well as harsh and vindictive.

Catherine's spirituality was mystical; it denoted direct experiential knowledge of God. Seeking the key to a holy dedicated life with uncommon attention and intensity, she learned the importance of self-knowledge, the development of personal virtue, and intimate personal knowledge of the divinity residing within her. The selflessness of unrestricted love which motivated her search brought about a transformation of her whole being. Catherine receded, and God became paramount; the love which motivated her became unrestricted compassion for God's people. To medievals, the indefinable essence, the inner power which drew people to her was a revelation of the mystic presence of God among them. Theologians of today acknowledge it to be the *conjunctio oppositorum*, the true mystical marriage in which the individual has become fully integrated, fully in tune with *anima* and *animus*, with body and spirit, with God and self. [30]

The mythic imagination of the middle ages lent itself to the language of mysticism. Symbolic images coming from the historic language of the Church, archetypal symbolism, symbols from nature, and from daily life were bound together with a practical homely expressiveness which created a new language, echoing from the recessed depths of the psyche.[31] The expressions Catherine used were pristine in their clarity. Visions took place in her own mind and understanding came through faith. This combination resulted in a knowledge, intuitive yet infused by the grace of the Spirit, which pierced the boundaries of human reason to touch the wisdom of the divine.

Such a gift drew the true mystic to the public domain. In every political or spiritual endeavor, true to her mystic vision, Catherine sought to effect change by the reform of the individual heart. She preached, not doctrinal decrees, but the new law, the example of Jesus Christ, which taught how to be, how to live, and how to practice the spirituality of the Beatitudes. Many holy women achieved degrees of status and recognition in this period; Catherine was the most outstanding, not only because of the breadth of her activity during her short life span of thirty-three years, but also because of her written legacy.

ENDNOTES

1. R. W. Southern characterized the medieval Church as "less than a state" because of its lack of coercive power, but in another sense much "more than a state." He wrote: "in the first place it was not and could never be simply, *a* state among many; it had to be *the* state or none at all. As soon as there were other states similarly equipped to rule, the Church was on its way to becoming a voluntary association for religious purposes." *Western Culture and the Church in the Middle Ages*, Penguin, Great Britain, 1977, p. 21.
2. Larner indicated the significance of this contest. "For the events at Agnani were in many ways merely the symbolic expression of the new relationship between the lay and ecclesiastical forces in Europe, the demonstration of the triumph of secular over ecumenical religious aims. These events merely pointed the obvious, that real papal control was a myth. . . . This brutal affirmation marked out a future in which real power lay with secular governments, and where they rather than the Church were to represent the values of society." *Culture and Society*, p. 55.
3. In addition to the personal consequences of being deprived of membership in the body of the Church, excommunication of a monarch released subjects from obligation to his rule; interdict was a punishment imposed upon a town, territory, or kingdom depriving the inhabitants of all the ordinary services of the Church except Baptism and Extreme Unction. In both instances, the purpose was to force submission to the law of the Church, but its only power was personal or public opinion.

4. The medieval perception of the difference in the two founders is borne out in Catherine's reference in the *Dialogue*: "Truly Dominic and Francis were two pillars of holy Church: Francis with the poverty that was his hallmark and Dominic with learning." (D. 158:340)
5. Southern, *Western Society*, pp. 46-47.
6. Marvin Becker, *Medieval Italy*, Indiana University Press, Bloomington, 1981, pp. 41-42.
7. For the reinterpretation of marriage and penance see ibid., pp. 31-34, 36-37; Baptism in Siena, and most towns of Italy, had more than a spiritual function since it also initiated the subject into membership in the commune.
8. In a letter from Catherine to Ristoro Canigiani, a devout layman who was a Florentine lawyer and leading politician of his city, we can see the type of spiritual direction which the laity of the time could accept. Regarding the reception of the Eucharist, she touched upon false humility versus true contrition, the immensity of God's love, and the Eucharist as food for the soul; her own grasp of the mystery — "all God and all Man" — and the depth of her faith is central to the direction she conveyed to this gentleman. "Now I answer you about the attitude we should hold toward Holy Communion, and how it befits us to take it. We should not use a foolish humility, as do secular men of the world. I say, it befits us to receive that sweet Sacrament, because it is the food of souls without which we cannot live in grace. . . . How ought we to receive it? With the light of most holy faith, and with the mouth of holy desire. In the light of faith you shall contemplate all God and all Man in that Host. Then the impulse that follows the intellectual perception, receives with tender love and holy meditation on its sins and faults, whence it arrives at contrition, and considers the generosity of the immeasurable love of God, who in so great love has given Himself for our food. Because one does not seem to have that perfect contrition and disposition which he himself would wish, he must not therefore turn away; for good will alone is sufficient. . . . I said that it does not befit us, nor do I wish you, to do as many imprudent laymen, who pass over what is commanded them by Holy Church, saying: 'I am not worthy of it.' Thus they spend a long time in mortal sin without the food of their souls. Oh, foolish humility! Who does not see that you are not worthy? At what time do you await worthiness? Do not await it; for you will be just as worthy at the end as at the beginning. For with all our just deeds, we shall never be worthy of it. But God is He who is worthy, and makes us worthy with his worth." Scudder, pp. 203-205.
9. See also Johnston, "Medieval Order of Penance," pp. 108-188. Once again, the general advice that Catherine gave Canigiani suggested, not just the intensity of Catherine's own devotional life, but devout exercises of prayer and penance common to the laity of her time, and appropriate to a man of Canigiani's position and stature: "Prayer must never be far from you. No, on the due and ordered hours, so far as you can, seek to withdraw a little, to know yourself, and the wrongs done to God, and the largess of His goodness, which has worked and is working so sweetly in you; opening the eye of your mind in the light of most holy faith, to behold how beyond measure God loves us; love which He shows us through the means of His only-begotten Son. And I beg that, if you are not saying it already, you should say every day the office of the Virgin, that she may be your refreshment and your advocate before God. As to ordering your life, I beg you to do it. Fast on Saturday, in reverence for Mary. And never give up the days commanded by Holy Church, unless of necessity. Avoid being at intemperate banquets, but live moderately, like a man who does not want to make a god of his belly. . . ." Scudder, p. 199.

10. Specific features marked individual groups, for example, the *Humiliati* engaged in public preaching and teaching. The unique feature of the Flagellants was the use of cords and chains to scourge their bodies, a common penitential monastic practice which they performed publicly and communally. Their motivation included individual as well as corporate goals: active participation in the Passion of Christ, personal repentance for sin, and expiation for the transgressions of all of Christendom. Eventually such groups gave way to the formation of multiple confraternities in the towns directed to acts of charity for one's neighbor, the reform of society, and of the Church. Following the outbreak of the Black Death in 1349, the Flagellants renewed these public penitential demonstrations with new vigor in response to this event which defied all human reason and control. In one dramatic gathering in Tournai, Belgium, the Dominican preacher who accompanied the hundreds of penitents described their demonstration as "the most noble effusion of blood since that of Christ himself." Unruly, indifferent to authority, the participants represented a mix of traditional piety and a new indifference to ordinary decorum which had an appeal to all classes of society. Southern, *Western Society*, p. 308; Becker, ibid., pp. 138-143.
11. Larner, *Age of Dante and Petrarch*, p. 235; Becker, ibid., pp. 145-146.
12. Southern, *Western Society*, p. 318; Larner, *Culture and Society*, p. 40; Becker, *Italy*, pp. 158-159.
13. Hook, *Siena*, p. 130.
14. Caroline Bynum, *Jesus as Mother: Studies in the Spirituality of the High Middle Ages*, University of California, Berkeley, 1982, pp. 16, 129; Becker, *Italy*, pp. 107-108, 122-123; Larner, *Age of Dante and Petrarch*, p. 246.
15. The significance of the artist as the teacher of the illiterate had a long history in the Church; Gregory the Great, emphasizing that painting was to the ignorant what writing was to the learned, had devised a symbolic representational system to convey meaning to the illiterate. In this later period, artists like Giotto led the way in emphasizing the humanity of Christ and the saints with a new naturalism, a three dimensional pictorial expressiveness which portrayed human emotions; art, now seen as presenting a symbolic language for the learned, conveyed layers and ranges of meaning. See for example, Larner, *Culture and Society*, pp. 44-45, 47-52.
16. See for example, Becker, *Italy*, pp. 37-38, 133.
17. See Pheme Perkins, "Biblical Traditions and Women's Experience," *America*, October 31, 1987, pp. 294-296 for Perkins' conclusion: "Women are allowed to do what is extraordinary and heroic when their witness preserves the tradition in times of challenge." p. 296. A correlation can be made to the alternation of roles of women during warfare in all secular societies.
18. Interest in women renowned from early Church tradition grew. Mary Magdalene was one of these, as were Saint Catherine of Alexandria, Saint Agnes, and Saint Barbara — all early martyrs. The year before Catherine's death, an altarpiece painted by Matteo di Giovanni was added to the Church of San Domenico, "Saint Barbara between Saint Catherine of Alexandria and Saint Mary Magdalene," a testament to the significance of these particular saints in the locale of Siena in Catherine's day. Such a climate of opinion made society ripe to accept women like Catherine of Siena in roles of public service. See Enzo Carli, *Sienese Painting*, New York Graphic Society, Greenwich, Conn., 1956, p. 66.
19. See Suzanne Wemple, *Women in Frankish Society*, University of Pennsylvania Press, 1981, chapters 7, 8.
20. *Illuminations of Hildegard of Bingen*, commentary by Matthew Fox, O.P., Bear and Company, New Mexico, 1985, p. 6.

21. Bynum, *Holy Feast*, p. 14; see also Barbara Newman, *Sister of Wisdom*, University of California Press, Berkeley, 1987 for a critical analysis of Hildegard's theology of the feminine.

22. A new climate of hostility was evident in the following statement by one of these Abbots. "We and our whole community of canons, recognizing that the wickedness of women is greater than all the other wickednesses of the world, and that there is no anger like that of women, and that the poison of asps and dragons is more curable and less dangerous to men than the familiarity of women, have unanimously decreed for the safety of our souls, no less than for that of our bodies and goods, that we will on no account receive any more sisters to the increase of our perdition , but will avoid them like the poisonous animals." Quoted in Southern, *Western Society*, p. 314.

23. Saint Bernard, a dominating figure in the Christian world of his day as well as the Cistercian Order, was famous for this anti-feminine advice to his monks. "To be always with a woman and not to have intercourse with her is more difficult than to raise the dead. You cannot do the less difficult; do you think I will believe you can do what is more difficult?" Quoted in ibid., p. 314.

24. Caroline Bynum has made a most significant contribution to scholarly study in the area of medieval holy women; chapter one of *Holy Feast and Holy Fast* provides a lucid and reliable overview of the question repeated as chapter 5, "Religious Women in the Late Middle Ages," in *Christian Spirituality*, Jill Raitt, ed., vol. 17 of *World Spirituality*, Ewert Cousins, gen. ed., Crossroad, New York, 1987. In her *Jesus as Mother*, the section on the Beguines is particularly helpful. Elizabeth Petroff, *Consolation of the Blessed*, Alta Gaia Society, New York, 1979, has provided a foundational interpretation of women visionaries of the period in a study indicating the common characteristics.

25. Southern, *Western Society*, p. 320; for graphs illustrating the growth of foundations from c. 1250-1400, see pp. 324-325.

26. Quoted in ibid., p. 330.

27. Bynum, *Jesus as Mother*, p. 172.

28. See, for example, *Meditations on the Life of Christ: An Illustrated Manuscript of the Fourteenth Century*, Isa Ragusa and Rosalie B. Green, eds., Princeton, New Jersey, 1959, for a type of meditational manual, copiously illustrated and introducing elaborate imaginary details and episodes which fleshed out the Gospel narrative with intimate and homely details. Originating in Italy, its wide appeal led to its being translated into many European languages, usually the vulgar tongues of the laity.

29. In Catherine's case, Dominican friars, Mantellate, and citizens who taunted her, accusing her of alliance with the devil, and of vainglory did not prevail, though this opposition was a painful and trying experience, a public testing of her patience, humility, charity, and forgiveness.

30. William Johnston, *The Mirror Mind*, Harper & Row, San Francisco, 1981, pp. 162-163.

31. Writing for a contemporary audience, William Johnston states, "Our increased knowledge of the unconscious, and our modern distinction between the ego and the self let us see that there can be movements in the psyche that are beyond our control. Such movements may look like the direct action of God when in fact they are movements of the unconscious and less known parts of our own psyche." *Being in Love*, p. 48. See also the author's *Silent Music: The Science of Meditation*, Harper & Row, San Francisco, 1974, pp. 73-74.

3

THE MEDIEVAL WORLD VIEW

Most biographies of late medieval saints begin with accounts of visionary experiences similar to Catherine of Siena's childhood vision. The frequency with which this occurs indicates the important place that assumptions about the power of vision, as an intermediary between the physical and the spiritual world, had in the medieval world view. Catherine's first biographer, Raymond of Capua, exemplified the medieval mindset in the life story through which we have come to know her. Her own writings also utilize the mythical language of symbolic iconography acceptable in her time. Therefore, any attempt to understand the spirituality of Saint Catherine of Siena must include an exploration of medieval ideas about God, society, sanctity, and the relationship with the divine which shaped both her personal vision and that of her world.

Neo-Platonic Thought

The world view which dominated medieval thought was a neo-Platonic one; that is, it was an imaginative mix of Plato's classical concepts of creation with newly developing Christian ideas. The result was a cosmology that assumed direct interaction between human, physical, and sense-oriented existence and a divine, imaginary, and spirit-oriented world. [1] Saint Augustine (354-430), primary among early Christian teachers and an enduring influence throughout the entire medieval period, laid the foundation for a Christian world view which emphasized the unity and interconnectedness of all creation. He declared that two cities — Jerusalem, the city of the love of God, and Babylon, the city of love of the world — were inseparable both here and in eternity. "Can we now separate them from each other?" he asked, only to respond in the negative: "They are thoroughly mixed together and from the very beginning of the human race they flow along, thoroughly mixed, even to the end of time."[2] Enduring from the fourth through the fifteenth centuries, this world view permeated religious and secular speculative thought to create a climate in which mysticism flourished.

Following Plato, the medieval cosmology depicted several distinct categories of existence. The divine was the highest realm of being, the non-corporeal. Human beings occupied a lower level, the corporeal, but could participate in the non-corporeal through the spiritual part of their being, the mind. In between these two was a world of spirits — good and evil — rejected neither by theology nor secular erudition.[3] Below these three was inanimate creation — stones and trees, for example — imprecise in definition, but considered to have power and energy to affect the living world. The link or "chain"[4] connecting all these levels of creation was "sight," a capacity of the mind.

Visual metaphors like "seeing," "looking at," and "gazing upon," became a vocabulary to express the interaction that medieval thinkers observed among the levels of being. In this way, "sight" became associated with creation, "looking at" meant bringing into being. When Macrobius (c. 360-c. 435), whose *Commentary on the Dream of Scipio* was the primary medieval exponent of the neo-Platonic schema, elaborated on the highest non-corporeal level of being, he explained that Mind flowed directly from God's own being. As long as Mind kept its "sight" fixed on God, it retained complete likeness to its Creator. When it "looked at" things below, Mind created Soul which, as a creation of Mind, retained a divine likeness if it kept its "gaze" fixed on God. [5]

The association of creating and visual perception led to an intellectual preoccupation with vision and sight that had a direct connection to the awe late medieval people had for mystics who transcended the limitations of human sight to see mystically. Similarly, this preoccupation gave rise to popular usage of a scholarly language laden with visual imagery and symbolic representation, a language essential to the mystic who spoke of what was seen in the mind.

Medieval Theories of Sight/Vision

Macrobius in his *Commentary* gave serious attention to the question of seeing and perceiving: his outline of neo-Platonic philosophy, already mentioned, contained an analysis of dreams. One of his five dream categories, a prophetic vision, is of special interest. [6] Both its designation as vision [*visio*] rather than dream [*somnium*] and its capacity for sight make this the most interesting of Macrobius' categories because it reveals the easy medieval interchange between vision and dream and asserts the capacity of sight to penetrate the unknown.

Augustine, Macrobius' contemporary, expanded this particular category of dreams by depicting three levels of sight directly reflecting the neo-Platonic conceptions of corporeal and non-corporeal. [7] Only the second occurred in sleep — though it was still categorized as vision; the other two suggested visions which transpired during periods of wakefulness. Corporal vision [*visio corporealis*], the ability to see disembodied matter with human eyesight, corresponded to the human corporeal level. Spiritual vision [*visio spiritualis* or *imaginativa*], the ability to see spiritual forms while sleeping, acknowledged the intermediary world of spirit-beings who could aid humans to attain the higher level. The highest form of intellectual vision [*visio intellectualis*], the direct human vision not only of bodiless beings but also of imageless concepts, indicated the access to the non-corporeal level enjoyed by a human through the noncorporeal mind.

Augustine consistently demonstrated his correspondence with the neo-Platonic world view. Listing the means God used to communicate with people, he included the corporeal, the spirit, and the inanimate worlds: the prophets, the angels, the written word, and the stars. Then, reflecting the highest divine level, he concluded, "Or God speaks directly to a person, not outwardly through one's ears, but inwardly in the mind."[8] Finally, in a major work, *De Trinitate*, Augustine portrayed the human mind as the most perfect created image of the Triune God because of its tripartite powers of memory, understanding, and will.[9]

Even eight hundred years after Augustine, deliberations about ways of seeing remained the subject of intellectual consideration. The Franciscan, Roger Bacon (1214-1294), considered the study of vision to be "the flower of all philosophy."[10] In a treatise on optics, he described three levels of vision directly patterned on the neo-Platonic model. Then, bridging the world of body and spirit with his proposition that the conditions of physical and spiritual sight are parallel, Bacon postulated that great saints were capable of attaining the direct vision attributed to God. Both Bacon's and Augustine's fascination with philosophical discussion of this nature contributed to a receptive intellectual atmosphere in which the mystic's vision was seen as a human transcendence of the barriers of the corporeal world to share in the likeness of God.

Artistic Symbolism

Developments in iconography, the visual symbolism of the artist, intensified the importance of sight and vision. As early as the sixth century, Pope Gregory the Great had encouraged painters to develop a visual vocabulary that would enable an illiterate laity to read art as the clergy read scripture. With the passage of time, the artist's visual imagery became a sophisticated language that spoke not only to the unlettered, but to the educated as well. Toward the end of the thirteenth century, the addition of precise directives aided understanding: bishops wore miters; abbots hoods; virgins carried lamps or lilies; and doctors of the Church held books in their hands. [11]

Encouraged by Church teaching, artists imitated the painter Giotto who had led the way in transforming verbal metaphors into concrete images that expressed spiritual qualities or relationships. In both painting and sculpture, virtues and vices were given symbolic forms which were instantly and universally recognizable. For example, in Ambrogio Lorenzetti's frescoes on good and bad government in the Palazzo Pubblico in Siena, Charity was instantly recognized by the heart in her outstretched hand, Faith by her cross, Justice by her scales, Wisdom by her book, and Peace by her olive branch.

All the faithful had a ready capacity to interpret symbols when new painting techniques added touching human portrayals of the Virgin and her Child with angels and saints and placed them in settings of naturalistic beauty. Later preaching styles intensified the significance of religious iconography by encouraging active use of the imagination before painted illustrations of God, the saints, and episodes from the Gospels. This meditational style deepened religious emotionality among all people who, consequently, were prepared to respect the mystics whose high degree of religious involvement led them to the naked experience of God in visions.

The Journey Metaphor

Similarly, legend and literature spanned the boundaries between the physical and spiritual worlds in stories recounting human efforts to arrive at the beatific vision. Early allegorical tales combined pagan, classical, and Christian elements preserved in oral tradition. Soon, they passed from legend to a written literature which recounted the human pursuit of a spiritual goal amid the landscape of the physical world. Even though this journey literature utilized secular, political, and spiritual themes, the language of their expression was highly symbolic.

For example, the Arthurian legends depicted one of the most popular of these journey metaphors: the knight's quest for the Holy Grail, the legendary cup used by Christ at the Last Supper. In sub-plots of this legend knights Gawain, Lancelot, Percival, and Galahad all pursued the Grail, with each personifying a different manner and degree of perfection — or a different level of vision — in their pilgrimage. Later, when knights participated in the spiritually motivated wars of the Crusades, they engaged in actual military expeditions, consecrated to their calling in a ceremony which resembled priestly ordination. Jerusalem, their actual destination, became entwined with a Jerusalem which, colored by imagination and pious legend, took on mystical and otherworldly meaning in the tradition of Augustine.

In religious stories of a highly mythical character monks and other holy persons engaged in journeys and pilgrimages in search of spiritual perfection, that is, union with God in the beatific vision. Common people, in their desire for assistance on their journeys, turned to the cult of the saints. Consequently, multitudes of medieval pilgrims travelled to holy places to make amends for their sins and to seek intercession by venerating holy relics. This popular practice resulted in a pilgrimage genre perfected in Chaucer's *Canterbury Tales*.

Many features, common to both physical and mythical journeys, illustrate unique medieval concepts of time and space. Time spanned from creation to the distant unknown future without any historical boundaries. Space, populated by corporeal, non-corporeal, and inanimate creation, indicated a sense of mystery, a sense of the existence of far more than could be seen with ordinary vision. Central to each journey story was the testing of the human spirit as danger came from one's own personal weakness or from visitations of threatening animal and spirit demons, but, angels or spiritual guides materialized to rescue the traveler. Descriptions of the treacherous and unexplored terrain that dominated the legends were speculative and reliant on scanty geographical knowledge; however, they shaped not only the stories, but also popular perceptions of lands foreign to personal experience. Ranging freely between reality and imagination, the journeys covered eons of time, translating historical persons and places from one period of history to another so that past events were interpreted with the insight of an observer from the present.

The journey's end was shrouded in mystery, ever compelling and ever fascinating in its provocative power. Apocryphal destinations depicted some meeting place of heaven and earth, of human and divine, of the imperfect and the perfect. Often, within sight of the goal that continually eluded the seeker, the traveler turned back from the brink of discovery with the realization that the world of the spirit must wait until death sealed the journey. Those who persevered to the goal but lacked the words to express the actuality of divine encounter, took refuge in silence or in death. Representing the best of medieval writing, Dante (1265-1321), in *The Divine Comedy*, is the ultimate example of the medieval seeker on journey. His visionary tour through the inferno of hell, the purgatory of waiting, and the paradise of the beatific vision contains all the common elements of medieval lore brought to perfection by a genius. Dante's journey also concludes in mystic silence as the beatific vision defies even his ability of expression.

Thus, attuned to the literature of journeys rife with symbolism, the medieval mind was equally receptive to accounts of

the spiritual journeys of mystics. Like the secular tales, the
terrain of their interior world was mysterious. Description defied
human language, necessitating the use of symbol and metaphor,
readily discernable to those accustomed to its meaning. Defined
in stages, the interior exploration increased gradually in intensity
and interiority. The human spirit, vigorously tested in encounters
with demons, was guided and strengthened by divine intervention. Total self-giving — a union of wills — preceded the realization of the mystic goal while the vision of God occurred in the
silence of an ecstatic trance that had all the physical appearances
of death.

The Legenda *of Raymond of Capua*

The life of Catherine of Siena which Raymond of Capua
wrote in the years immediately following her death quite naturally
reflects the world view of his time. As it had with Macrobius,
Augustine, and Bacon before him, the neo-Platonic cosmology
shaped his world view. Pivotal in his spirituality, as in that of
Catherine, was the interconnectedness between the physical and
spiritual worlds, the influence of good and bad spirits, and the
essential significance of vision as the integrating element in the
ordering of all things. Consequently, the biography that he wrote
falls into the category of hagiography because Raymond, coming
out of this climate of opinion, emphasized the mythical and
miraculous elements favored by his intellectual formation.

Christians of the fourteenth century expected confessors of
holy women to idealize them in death in a biography which would
promote the process of their canonization. [12] A trained theologian
and scholar, Raymond was intellectually well suited to record
Catherine's life; he entitled it a *Legenda* to indicate, in the par-
lance of his day, a life story to be read aloud. However, recounting Catherine's life experience in a manner that would be histori-

cally truthful and render her worthy of canonization required that Raymond also authenticate a new mode of female sanctity within the accepted definitions of the day. To a Church no longer suffering from persecution, the earlier ideal of the virgin-martyr experience was no longer a viable one.

Medieval religious practice had adopted heroic patience, devotion to the Passion of Christ, an extreme sense of sinfulness and penitence, and a mystic's direct perception of God in place of the heroism of martyrdom. [13] Raymond, like others in his position, would emphasize these characteristics which were so meaningful to his time and culture, often drawing conscious parallels between Catherine and saints revered by her contemporaries. Portraying her in the image of earlier heroic women such as Mary Magdalene and Catherine of Alexandria added an aura to her story, which was readily acceptable to the medieval mind though foreign to a present day understanding of human nature.

The Golden Legends of Voragine laid the foundation for a popular ideal of sanctity giving rise to medieval type-models of perfection and promoting a view of sanctity intended not so much as *imitanda* but as *admiranda*, not to be imitated but to provoke the reader or listener to awe, wonder, and admiration. Gradually, the *Legends* inspired and colored the writing of life histories like Catherine's so that, identified with the sanctity portrayed by popular saints, she would be seen readily as worthy of canonization.

An intimate friend, a privileged confidant, a companion and witness to much of the final six years of her public life, Raymond underscored his close relationship with his subject by frequent personal references interspersed in the text. For example, we read: "the memory of her words is truly a great comfort to me in times of sadness and discouragement" (L. 307); "true it was I could no longer enjoy her holy conversation" (L. 308); "Fearful at the thought of losing her so soon" (L. 276); and "I and all the other Friars who were spiritually regenerated by her." (L. 112) Because of this personal relationship, Raymond included much that was human in his presentation of Catherine.[14] However, because of his ready acceptance of the miraculous and his overriding urge to present her as holy, Raymond dramatized the marvelous to raise Catherine above the realm of ordinary human sanctity.[15] Indeed, the closing statement of the text proclaims his purpose. "All things considered, it can be said that the name of this saint, virgin and martyr should be recorded by the Church Militant in the catalogue of the Saints. . . ." (L. 384)

It was important to Raymond to show examples of divine favor toward Catherine in order to present her as an immediate agent of divine power.[16] Therefore, he placed tremendous significance on incidents of ecstasy in Catherine's life which he saw as "the foundation, root, and origin of all her holy deeds and the tangible evidence of her admirable inner life." (L. 74) Portraying incidents from her religious experience, he freely used the metaphorical language common to his period without transitional explanation. For example, he seems to have Catherine actually take her heart out of her body and remain three days without a human heart until Christ gives her his own. (L. 165) In truth, this action reflects the artistic symbolism used by Giotto and Lorenzetti, when Charity holds its heart out to represent the human giving of one's total self to God.[17] He frequently used these symbolic artistic devices of his world as if they were concrete experience. He describes in detail a marriage ceremony, in reality a mystical marriage, as if it actually happened; this symbolism, an archetypal image of the most intimate union between a human being and God, was a popular theme in religious painting of the day.[18]

In addition to advancing Catherine's canonization, the *Legenda* promoted the Dominican Order and the papacy of Urban VI, whose legitimacy was threatened by the Great Schism. Raymond initiated the writing of the *Legenda* five years after Catherine's death during his term as Master General of the portion of the Order which supported Urban VI's claim. This remnant was further splintered by Raymond's introduction of reform measures intended to return the friars to the original fervor and charism of Saint Dominic. Each of these causes had been of deep significance to Catherine during her lifetime. The support of the Urbanist Papacy occupied all her final energies, and the reform of the "mystic body of Holy Church" was, perhaps, primary among all her public concerns. Raymond's impulse to restore Dominican fervor was a direct response to her spiritual influence.

It is not unusual, then, that in the *Legenda* Raymond would seek to advance these efforts by validating the sanctity of one whose life had been dedicated to their fulfillment while she lived. Catherine, willing to be an instrument for the Church, papacy, and Dominican Order in her lifetime, would smile upon the strengthening of these institutions with her life story. In one of her final letters she gave permission to Raymond and a few of her most trusted disciples to use their judgment in the disposition of her writings:

> I ask you too, as regards the book [*Dialogue*] and any other writing of mine you find . . . to go through them and to do with them whatever you see to be most to God's honor. . . .[19]

In the third section of his text, Raymond makes repeated references to Catherine's devoted service to the papacy under both Gregory XI and Urban VI. He emphasizes her stand on the schism as identical to his own; for example, she is quoted as stating, "Urban is the true vicar of Christ, whatever the slanderous schismatics may say." (L. 307) To illustrate that Catherine's association with Saint Dominic and the Dominican Order was divinely inspired, Raymond gave several examples from her childhood. He told of a youthful "vision" of Saint Dominic after which Catherine "suddenly developed such a high idea of this Order that whenever she saw any of the Preaching Friars going past the house she would watch where they put their feet and then as soon as they had gone by go and kiss their footprints. . . ." (L. 33) At one point, "she made it a rule to stay awake every night while the Preaching Friars . . . slept," watching in prayer for them until the friars arose. (L. 71) In a pivotal "dream," in which Dominic appeared with other founders of religious orders, under divine inspiration Catherine was drawn to desire the Dominican habit. (L. 47) Dominic was also one of four holy witnesses to Catherine's later visionary betrothal ceremony. (L. 99)

Raymond worked carefully, but within the limits of his medieval concept of hagio/biography. While he was an actual participant only during the concluding six years of Catherine's life, many of her experiences, especially those concerning the development of her inner life, were known to him from intimate and privileged conversation. From interviews with eye witnesses, he culled information about Catherine's early life. Moreover, he had access to her *Dialogue*, to parts of her correspondence, especially to the letters addressed to him in which she freely revealed her personal life. However, even in these circumstances, historians must consider hagiographical "facts" as only "perceptions" which require careful interpretation to recognize the purpose and intention of the writer. [20] This approach underlies the importance of a fresh interpretation for people of a different time and culture.

As a hagiographer, Raymond's perception of sanctity, "primarily miraculous rather than exemplary," caused him to present Catherine as one who performed miracles and attracted divine favor, therefore, as one "qualitatively different from other believers."[21] Though he portrayed Catherine with virtuous characteristics common to ordinary Christians — prayerfulness, patience, and charity, for example — this suggestion of imitable qualities is quite overpowered by the cumulative effect of incidents requiring admiration.

Raymond accomplished the task that he set himself in a superb manner, for Catherine emerges from the *Legenda* as a saint recognizable to her own medieval generation. The sanctity he portrayed was anticipated by laity, clerics, and papal authorities, formed and shaped by the saints popularized in *The Golden Legends.* But Catherine's account of her experience, *The Dialogue,* differs from Raymond's version and from the fictional literature mentioned above in that it is an autobiographical record. As such, it is relevant to historical interpretation even though Catherine's language like the language of the literature is symbolic and like that of Raymond, it incorporates the iconographic vocabulary of her time period.

One realizes, then, that Catherine's spirituality is representative of a commonly held medieval world view, and her journey to union with God, her transcendence from the human level to that of the divine, is accomplished through her noncorporeal mind and soul. According to the neo-Platonic custom, she makes clear distinctions regarding the levels of consciousness which constitute her experiences. Some incidents, clearly occurring in sleep, she labels dreams; others, experienced while awake, she describes as taking place in her "mind's eye"; finally, to indicate a higher category of revelation, she speaks of what she sees with "the eye's pupil, most holy faith."[22]

People of Catherine's time period were responsive to a religious expression and to a sanctity which embraced the mystical experience. The simple as well as the powerful and the well-educated openly sought the company of those who had penetrated the mystery of God. Thus, the influence which mystics like Catherine of Siena exerted was the result of a general fascination with the spirit world following from the popular understanding of the neo-Platonic chain of created being. Willingness to believe that humans could penetrate to a divine level of consciousness caused both the humble and the mighty to seek out the mystic as a disseminator of the direct wisdom of divine inspiration. Catherine's time, then, was a fertile one for the mystic voice to be heard.

ENDNOTES

1. For the framework of this chapter, see Carolly Erickson, *The Medieval Vision*, Oxford University Press, New York, 1976, Chapters 1-2.
2. *Accounts of the Psalms*, Ps. 64-65:1-2. Quoted in *Dictionary of the Middle Ages*, ed., Joseph Strayer, Scribner's, New York, 1982, "Augustine of Hippo," Edward Synan, I, pp. 646-659, p. 654.
3. Though the Church opposed sorcery, the use of charms, and all forms of superstition, theologians accepted the existence of a spirit world which Saint Jerome, for example, declared to be multitudinous.
4. Macrobius, in *Commentary on the Dream of Scipio*, tr. & ed. by William Harris Stahl, Columbia University Press, New York, 1952, p. 145, refers to the golden chain related in Homer, a chain which God ordered hung between the sky and the earth to hold all creation in balance and order [*Iliad*, 8, 19].
5. Ibid., p. 143. Macrobius declares that "no one denies" that the mind "is more divine than soul." The mind, he says, is the essence that we have in common with the sky and the stars, while the soul is imprisoned within the confines of the body, "to which the divine mind is not subject."
6. Macrobius described five dream categories, two of which, nightmare [*insomnium*] and apparitions [*visum*], were figments of the mind of the dreamer in the early stages of sleep. The other three represented possible guides to conduct and/or aids in foretelling the future. In an oracular dream [*oraculum*], a person might appear, tell of the future and advise the dreamer; an enigmatic dream [*somnium*] conveyed a message concealed in ambiguity. The final type, a prophetic vision [*visio*] contained direct glimpses of the future. Ibid., pp. 87-91.
7. Augustine makes these remarks in a commentary on II Corinthians 12:2-4 to explicate Paul's visionary experience of being raised to the third heaven. *The Literal Meaning of Genesis*, 2 vol., Num. 42, *Ancient Christian Writers*, tr. by John Hammond Taylor, S.J., Newman Press, II, Book Twelve, pp. 178-231.
8. Sermons (12:4).
9. *The Trinity*, McKenna, ed., vii, xi.
10. Erickson, pp. 43-45.
11. Larner, *Culture and Society*, pp. 43-45.
12. Sainthood had ceased to be a popular declaration by a town or community of its local holy person; canonization had become a papal process requiring a rigorous examination. However, Catherine's canonization (1461) occurred during the papacy of Pope Pius II, a member of the Sienese Piccolomini family, indicating the lingering influence of local popular appeal in the canonization of medieval saints.
13. Richard Kieckhefer, *Unquiet Souls: Fourteenth Century Saints and Their Religious Milieu*, University of Chicago Press, Chicago, 1984, pp. 18-19.
14. One rule of thumb in the evaluation of hagiographical evidence is that the more a biographer departs from a classical description of virtue with the addition of personal details and familial information to underlay the uniqueness of the saint, the more surely historians can rely on the material. The wealth of this type of personal and family detail in the *Legenda* is carefully verified, especially when Raymond recounts incidents which he did not personally witness. See Weinstein and Bell, p. 13.
15. See a detailed evaluation in John Coakley, "The Representation of Sanctity in late Medieval Hagiography: Evidence from *Lives* of Saints of the Dominican Order," unpublished doctoral thesis, Harvard Divinity School, 1980, chapter 3, pp. 51-106.

16. Coakley, p. 45. In addition to the *Legenda*, Raymond was also the author of the *Legenda Agnetis*, a life of Agnes of Montepulciano completed in 1365, thirty years previous to his composition of Catherine's life. Agnes was deceased when Raymond, assigned as director to the monastery at Montepulciano, gathered the fragments of her life story into a formal account. This experience with direction and study of holy women is believed to have been a factor influencing the choice of Raymond as spiritual advisor and protector of Catherine.

17. Giotto initiated this symbolism in the Arena Chapel in Padua; a female, labeled Charity, extends her heart in her hand to Christ, pictured in the upper right corner of the frame: Meiss, fig. 109. This representation of a spiritual expression become a concrete image also appears in Ambrogio Lorenzetti's "Allegory of Good Government," Carli, plate 71, detail.

18. This expression of the unitive state began to appear in thirteenth and fourteenth century painting as marriage ceremonies: the Virgin Mary and her Son, Saint Francis of Assisi and Lady Poverty, and most importantly for Catherine's legend, Saint Catherine of Alexandria and Jesus. Raymond described an elaborate visionary ceremony in which Catherine was betrothed to Christ; immediately, he likened her experience to that of Catherine of Alexandria, a model instantly recognized by his audience. (L. 100) See Meiss, fig. 99, 102, 100, 105, 106, 107.

19. *I, Catherine*, Letter 60, p. 270.

20. Weinstein and Bell, p. 8.

21. Coakley, pp. 90, 105.

22. Raymond's failure to distinguish between a wakeful vision and a sleeping dream demonstrates his position of recorder of another's experience. His language, however, is consistent with the metaphorical content of medieval painting. See, for example, "The Vision of Saint Joachim," a fresco painted by Giotto for the Arena Chapel in Padua, which portrays Saint Joachim asleep; an angel in the painting signifies that God is communicating to Joachim in a dream. Eimerl, p. 118. In Pietro Lorenzetti's altarpiece, "Sabac's Dream," a man is sleeping in a bed chamber as an angel hovers over him; again, the symbolism implies that God is speaking to a dreamer. Carli, Plate 55.

4

THE AUTOBIOGRAPHICAL RESOURCES

In pictorial images dating from the late fourteenth century Catherine is shown holding a red book in her hand, the *Dialogue*. Since in the common iconographic symbolism used by artists, a book indicated a saint who was a Doctor of the Church,[1] its presence in paintings of the period suggests that Catherine was popularly accorded this honor by her own generation in recognition of her eminence as a teacher and writer. Only belatedly was this status made official. After all of Catherine's writings had been examined and found free of doctrinal error, she became, together with Saint Teresa of Avila, one of the two women declared a Doctor of the Church in 1970.

The substance of Catherine's life and her connection to her own historic environment is most clearly evident in these writings. Though not intended as autobiography, the abundance of personal anecdote and experiential description which color them have earned her a literary reputation as a "biographer and painter of herself."[2] Her *Letters* give evidence to the wide audience she reached and to the teaching and guidance that she customarily gave. Her *Prayers*, revealing the concerns foremost in her mind, portray the language and the attitude with which she customarily approached God. Her lengthy *Dialogue* of conversation between herself and God, which details the process of her own interior development, is an inclusive summary of her teaching. The themes explicated in all three sources coincide and overlap. In many cases the *Dialogue* echoes ideas already formulated in the

Letters while the *Prayers* reiterate both the *Letters* and the *Dialogue.*

Catherine's complete writings rest on a dual foundation: traditional Church teaching and a mystic's direct and unmediated knowledge of God and God's way of dealing with humanity. That part of Catherine's *Dialogue* which is rational and systematic and the portions of her *Letters* and *Prayers* which have a hortatory and instructional quality demonstrate her Dominican formation, geared to preaching and teaching. On the other hand, Catherine's writings are also a unique and creative exposition of her direct relationship with God.

Because of her background, Catherine is intellectually rooted in the long tradition of mystical theology dating back to ancient Greek philosophy as it was reformulated in the teachings of the Christian Church in both East and West. However, she speaks while lost in a transport of love to reveal the power, the wisdom, and the mercy of God. Thus, her testament has an intense and dramatic personal quality. However, it is her habitual use of symbols to convey meaning, a device typical of mystics and of the literary expression of her time, that lends a timelessness to her story because metaphor provides an inclusive language decipherable in every age. [3]

Though Catherine borrows many symbols from a long historic tradition, her treatment of them is profoundly integrative in its layering and confirms the harmony of her intellect and spirituality. She communicates with a creative power that is both rhythmic and generative, causing her symbols to transcend conventional interpretation. With the fluidity characteristic of mystic insight, she constantly reaches for the infinite, using language with the dynamism of a painter's brush alive in the hand of a master artist. Continually shaping, forming, and expanding, she focuses meaning, then layers on new images that communicate higher levels of interpretation. [4] The tree of virtue gives way to the tree of the cross, for example, while climbing the stairs carved out of Christ's suspended body becomes a continuous spiralling process in which her rational powers — memory, understanding, and will — gradually become one harmonious functioning unit.

Many commonalities connect Catherine to other mystics. Love of God is central, and the goal of the relationship is an intimate encounter between the human and the divine person. She emphasizes the unity of the Godhead, teaching that the human is to reflect that unity by bringing its memory, understanding, and will to a oneness which will mirror the three in one of the divine Trinity. The symbolism which cloaks her account describes an ascent through three progressive stages which lead her from the level of human weakness to a higher spiritual one. Light is a symbol of a growing purification of her understanding until, infused with divine wisdom, it leads her at last to unity with the Beloved. Love which leads to such union, progress through three spiritual stages, and the necessity of divine guidance by enlightenment are common threads in all mystical writing.

The Letters

Catherine's letters were dictated to secretaries. Consequently, they have a style intended to exhort, to teach, and to call the recipient to virtue. Ordinarily, Catherine responds to letters received; however, at times, she assumes the initiative. For example, when involved in papal crises, she does not hesitate to write to political and religious leaders whose support appears crucial to her view of the well-being of the Church.

Typically, Catherine frames her message in a symbol. For example, in a letter to the parish priest of Asciano who does not meet her high standards of conduct, she begins by asking him to be "the fragrant flower you ought to be, breathing out a sweet perfume in God's gracious presence."[5] Meticulously, she elaborates her image, preparing the recipient to appreciate the point she wishes to make. In this case, it is one of personal reformation so she describes the flower left standing so long in water that it gives off a fetid odor rather than a fragrance. Then, in the body of the letter, she addresses the issue at hand with details of what must be corrected before she returns to her image. The closing expresses her desire for the individual; she urges in this instance, that the priest change his way of life and begin to breathe out a sweet fragrance, as a flower should, for the people entrusted to his care.

As an autobiographical resource, the *Letters* provide an interpretive tool to supplement the *Dialogue*. Catherine's symbolism embellishes and clarifies the meaning of the same ideas when they appear in the *Dialogue*.

The Prayers

Catherine's habit of praying aloud in the presence of her followers gave rise to a collection of twenty-six prayers recorded from a lifetime of prayer. The fact that the earliest ones date from her stay at Avignon suggests that her followers, led by Raymond, were aware of the historic significance of Catherine's presence there and sought to document it. The final twenty prayers of the collection represent the Roman period, the last fourteen months of her life. Both the tone and content of these later prayers suggest an underlying motivation to teach her "family" as Catherine becomes aware of her weakened capacity and conscious of her impending death. These prayers frequently restate ideas and beliefs, symbols and images, concerns and directives already familiar to her followers, and encapsulate the more lengthy instruction in the *Letters* and *Dialogue*.

Though frequently the prayers have a narrative quality, editorial comment indicates that long pauses interrupted the flow of words when Catherine was drawn into the silence of mystic contemplation. This silence conceals the essential encounter of intimate communion with God although the recorded fragment provides a unique opportunity to probe Catherine's image of God and her view of herself in relation to God. Her conversation with God, even in the presence of witnesses, is intensely personal, sincere, and self revealing; therefore, the *Prayers* provide additional insight into the flesh and blood Catherine.

A prayer recorded on the journey home from Avignon illustrates her approach to the prayer of petition. (P. 3:35-39) Following a private meeting in Genoa with an already discouraged Gregory, Catherine offers prayer for him. Beginning with praise, she addresses the Father as all-powerful, eternal God, as boundless most gentle charity, and finally, as the way, the truth, and the life. This last metaphor for the path to Heaven hammered out by Christ's redemptive sacrifice will be her theme; as in the letters, she frames each prayer in an integrating symbol.

She speaks of the Son's obedient acceptance of the Father's will "in anxiety, poverty, and anguish" even to the "bitter death of the cross." The redemptive mission of the Son is then likened to the task set before Gregory, the vicar of Christ on earth, who must also endure toil, deprivation, anxiety, and peril to redeem those whose disobedience to the Church has cut them off from salvation. She speaks of those weak advisors of his whose "presumptuous judgment and fleshly motivation" would deter the vicar from doing his duty; she speaks as well of the immense responsibility placed upon Gregory and how he should rejoice to do God's will.

Consequently, Catherine prays and beseeches "your most holy mercy" that Gregory will be purified and made to burn with desire to win back the lost souls. "And if his dallying displeases you," she prays, "punish my body for it, for I offer and return it to you to scourge and ravage as you please." Catherine continues to outline her wishes for the pontiff as she extols the great love and mercy of God for his people. She closes, as is her custom, with a petition for her own followers, "these servants of yours who are present here," that they may follow God's will "which alone is purity, which alone is eternal and everlasting," concluding, "And for all of them I give you thanks."

In the midst of her petition, Catherine takes time to offer continuous praise. God is love incomprehensible, infinite goodness and boundless charity. He is eternal compassion, one who in mercy and unutterable grace has fallen in love with what he has made. She permits her imagination to flow freely; the whole of Christ's redemption drama is one with the plight of the Church, of the papacy, and of those humans enmeshed in the conflicting loyalties of Church and state. In Catherine's prayer, spiritual and public responsibilities are inseparably united in the one divine will.

The Dialogue

Scholars generally accept the fact that the underlying plan of the *Dialogue* came to Catherine in ecstatic prayer shortly after her return from Avignon in the fall of 1377. Pope Gregory XI's return to Italy initiated such a variety of new problems that political and social unrest intensified, threatening to overwhelm his good will. Catherine, meanwhile, resided with the Salimbeni family in an outlying area of Siena called Rocca d'Orcia. Raymond, having been dispatched to Rome with Catherine's suggestions and plans for peace, had been permanently detained there by an appointment as Prior of the Dominican Church of Santa Maria sopra Minerva.

Catherine soon became aware of an estrangement between herself and Pope Gregory. Communication between them was cut off, even through Raymond, and prospects for the peace which she desired for all of Italy and for the Church swiftly deteriorated.[6] Isolated from these central events, powerless to intervene, unable to go to Rome unless summoned, Catherine remained at Rocca d'Orcia. This was a time of deep internal suffering. The certitude of purpose which had previously motivated and energized her began to erode while painful self-doubt raised questions of her understanding of the mission entrusted to her.[7]

Eventually, two letters arrived from Rome; one from Raymond and another from Gregory broke the silence of alienation.[8] Renewal of contact so restored Catherine's spirit that, in the deep mystical prayer that followed, the germ of the *Dialogue* emerged. She confirms this sequence of events at the beginning of the *Dialogue* as well as in a letter to Raymond:

> And she had on her mind, besides, a letter she had received from her spiritual father, a letter in which he expressed pain and unbearable sadness over the offense against God, the damnation of souls, and the persecutions against holy Church. (D. 2:27)

> When I thoroughly understood your letters, I begged a servant of God [herself] to offer tears and sweats before God, for the Bride [the Church] and because of "Babbo's" [Pope Gregory's] weakness. . . .[9]

This letter to Raymond continued with a short formulation of what would eventually become the *Dialogue*: four petitions followed by divine responses. The first petition was for herself since she knew she could not help others unless she had personally attained and confirmed herself in virtue; the second was for the reform of holy Church, the third was for the whole world, with special reference to those who lacked peace because of their rebellion against the Church; and the fourth was for a special case, a person in great need whose identification has not been determined with certitude. (D. 1:26)

This mystic prayer, an intense experience of centering to a

profound personal depth, was accompanied by a resolve to enter
into Christ's Passion. Catherine began to think of herself as an
expiatory sacrifice for the good of her neighbor and for the reform
and purification of the Church, a goal which up to that time had
eluded her prayers, words, and deeds. Again, this is confirmed
both in the *Dialogue* and in her correspondence with Raymond:

> I accuse myself before you, asking that you punish my sins
> in this life. And since I by my sins am the cause of the
> sufferings my neighbors must endure, I beg you in mercy to
> punish me for them. (D. 2:27)

> Soul mine, you have wasted your whole life. Therefore
> have so great losses and evils fallen on the world and on
> Holy Church, in general and particular. So now I wish you to
> atone with sweat of blood. [10]

Thus the *Dialogue*, initiated at this crucial turning point of
her life, was more than a testament of her life and teaching for the
instruction and edification of her followers. Catherine connected
to her own inner power and authority and took control of her own
experience; she clarified for herself, as well as for others, God's
action in her life. In this way, she overcame the sense of failure
which threatened her and returned her inner and outer life to
harmony.

The structure that she chose, a dialogue, was a popular
medieval form. Learned men typically engaged in intellectual
disputation with a disciple while learned medieval women typically dialogued with God. [11] Obviously, Catherine was aware of
this different cultural standard and chose the feminine form. She
prayed intermittently as she made her petitions, but the divine
voice predominated as God responded to her.

The relational attitude is clear. Catherine is the seeker, the
petitioner, the one in need while God is First Truth, the reposit-
ory of all that is. Since the profound essence of Catherine's

teaching on self-knowledge is that it can only be achieved within the knowledge of God, any exposition of herself would, of necessity, be a revelation of God. Therefore, God is teacher in the dialogue between them.

In a letter to her closest female friend, Alessa dei Saracini, Catherine declared that these two kinds of knowledge, of self and God, needed to "be seasoned with the other and made into one and the same thing."[12] This expression exemplifies the foundational significance of self-knowledge as the means of knowing God in all of Catherine's life and teaching. Unlike Raymond's *Legenda*, in the *Dialogue*, neither Catherine's sanctity, her admirable virtue, her miraculous interventions, nor her public successes figure; only the human person standing in the presence of God is relevant.

Her style, described as "layer on layer of interwoven development,"[13] affirms Catherine's perception that progress in the spiritual life is one of continuous growth: sequential, gradual, and ordered in stages. The content reveals the importance of repeated experiences which, with the gift of faith, occur and recur, discerned with ever deepening meaning and wisdom.[14] The unique flavor of Catherine's self-revelation is apparent in the opening petition in which her freedom to express the essence of herself is revealed. We know intuitively that this is a woman who has encountered and seeks to enter even deeper into her own authentic core:

> A soul rises up, restless with tremendous desire for God's honor and the salvation of souls. She has for some time exercised herself in virtue and has become accustomed to dwelling in the cell of self-knowledge in order to know better God's goodness toward her, since upon knowledge follows love. And loving, she seeks to pursue truth and clothe herself in it.
>
> But there is no way that she can so savor and be

enlightened by this truth as in continual humble prayer, grounded in the knowledge of herself and of God. For by such prayer the soul is united with God, following in the footsteps of Christ Crucified, and through desire and affection and the union of love he makes of her another himself. (D. 1:25)

ENDNOTES

1. This symbolism was devised for artists by Guillaume Durand in the late 1300's. See Larner, *Culture and Society*, pp. 48-49.

2. de Santis, p. 124.

3. See Maurice Nicoll, *The New Man*, Shambhala, Boston, 1986, pp. 2-3 for an explication of parabolic language; for example, "The idea behind all sacred writing is to convey a higher meaning than the literal words contain. . . . This meaning must be concealed, as it were, by an outer wrapping." Today, psychologists recognize that symbolic language serves a mediating function, making accessible to consciousness what is inaccessible to direct sensory experience and to reason. See Anne Belford Ulanov, *The Feminine in Jungian Psychology and in Christian Theology*, Northwestern University Press, Evanston, 1971, p. 21.

4. Ordinary language fails the mystic who endeavors to recount her experience. Catherine prays in the *Dialogue*, "And what shall I say? I will stutter, 'A —,' because there is nothing else I know how to say. Finite language cannot express the emotion of the soul who longs for you infinitely. I think I could echo Paul's words; The tongue cannot speak nor the ear hear nor the eye see nor the heart imagine what I have seen!" (D. 153:325-326) The difficulty experienced in finding words to express a meeting with God is reiterated two hundred years later by Saint John of the Cross. "Not only does a man feel unwilling to give expression to this wisdom, but he finds no adequate means or similitude to signify so sublime an understanding and delicate a spiritual feeling. Even if the soul should desire to convey this experience in words and think up many similitudes, the wisdom would always remain secret and still to be experienced." John of the Cross, *Dark Night of the Soul*, II:17:3.

5. *Letters*, 10, p. 56. Images may have a different focus depending on the message; hence, Catherine sometimes dictated more than one letter at a time tailoring the symbolism to the need of the individual.

6. Letters to encourage Raymond, also denied access to the papal presence, reveal the source of her own strength in the face of suffering and torment, "God has provided and shall provide, and His providence shall not be lacking." Ever perceptive, she described the political climate of the papal court, "if from men religious or secular, even in the mystical body of Holy Church, you have suffered persecution or displeasure, or have been visited with the indignation of the Vicar of Christ, either on your own account, or if you have had something to bear on my account with all these people — you are not to resist, but bear it patiently." She requested Raymond to deliver to the Pope a message in which her self-doubt poured out in self-accusation.

Continuing, however, she quickly shifted from the stance of humble servant to that of formidable advisor as she reminded Gregory of his duty to restore order to Italy and the Church. "I hope in the goodness of God and in your holiness that what is not done you will do. . . . God demanded that you do this — as you know you were told — that you care for the reformation of Holy Church, punishing its sins and establishing good shepherds; and that you make peace with your wicked sons in the best way and most pleasing to God that could be done. . . ." Scudder, pp. 337, 339.

7. She confided something of this painful time to Alessa dei Saracini, "apparently my Bridegroom, Eternal Truth, has wished to put me to a very sweet and genuine test, inward and outward, in the things which are seen and those which are not — the latter beyond count the greater. . . . The pain of lacking consolations from my fellow-creatures has called me to consider my own lack of virtue, recognizing my imperfection, and the very perfect light of Sweet Truth . . . I beg you . . . do not slacken in prayer for me; no, redouble it — for I have greater need than you see. . . . For my life is of very little use to anyone else; rather it is painful and oppressive to every person, far and near, by reason of my sins." Scudder, pp. 231-232.

8. These letters are not part of the surviving legacy.

9. Scudder, p. 337.

10. Ibid, p. 339.

11. A dialogue was a popular and effective medieval intellectual device to convey teachings. In their dialogues both Augustine and Gregory the Great carried on "disputations" with a disciple. Women, for example, Hildegard of Bingen and Hadewijch the Flemish Beguine, like Catherine seemingly excluded from the male role of disputant, chose to dialogue with God. Christine de Pisan in the fifteenth century broke this feminine tradition when she dialogued with three virtues appearing to her in female form. These were reason, integrity, and justice — virtues typically the preserve of men.

12. *I, Catherine*, Letter 33, p. 151.

13. *Dialogue*, Introduction, pp. 9-10.

14. See Nicoll, pp. 3-4 for an interpretation of the inner psychological development of the understanding, and "that man internally is a seed capable of definite growth." See also William Barry, S.J., "Surrender: The Key to Wholeness," *Review for Religious*, 46 (Jan./Feb., 1987), pp. 49-53, in which Barry writes of the cyclical nature of the spiritual life. ". . . even if we do achieve a new level of trust in God and freedom from our past, we will once again be tempted to make an idol of this new identity, this new God-experience, and the cycle will begin all over. That is our lot as human beings." pp. 52-53.

PART TWO

TO MIRROR THE TRINITY: CATHERINE'S INNER WORLD

Catherine's first call, her vision in the sky over San Domenico at the age of six, marked her indelibly. (L. 25) This mental image, seen in her "mind's eye" as she walked the streets of her native Siena, was a visual parable; its setting and the personages indicated her life vocation. The bridal chamber and Jesus' loving glance invited the relationship of a spouse, while his pontifical attire and the presence of Peter the first Pope called her to consecrate herself to the service of the Church. Her work would entail the preaching and teaching of a Paul and the contemplative relationship patterned on that of Jesus and John the beloved disciple. These components exemplified a Dominican vocation: contemplation that would bear the fruit of an active ministry of service to the Church through preaching and teaching. Catherine's integration of these elements in her childhood vision suggests her precocious intelligence as well as the pervasive influence of Dominican spirituality in this very early stage of her religious formation.[1]

The visionary scene ignited hope in Catherine's youthful heart, troubled as it was by the thought that her future would resemble that of her newly married sister Bonaventura whose unhappy home she had just visited. (L. 20) Her desire for security, perceived in the promise of God having a purpose for her, drew Catherine away from society into solitude. Though her youth precluded her discerning its inner meaning with mature insight, the vision, nevertheless, evoked an enthusiasm that sustained her throughout her lifetime.

At the age of twenty-nine, a more spiritually mature Catherine told of another vision; this one drew her to immerse herself in the public turmoil of her medieval world. Her concern with the violence and unrest which surrounded her, with rebellions against the Church, and with injustice in Church administration had become the focus of her prayer. She described in a letter to Raymond and a group of followers how, on the night of April 1, 1376, she had an experience in which God "showed his marvels" to her so that her "soul seemed to be outside" her body and was "so overwhelmed with joy" that words failed to describe it. Then, as "the fire of holy desire" grew in her, she saw in her mind's eye streams of people entering the side of Christ crucified.

> In desire and impelled by love I walked through their midst and entered with them into Christ gentle Jesus. And with me were my father Saint Dominic, the beloved John, and all my children. Then he placed the cross on my shoulder and put the olive branch in my hand, as if he wanted me (and so he told me) to carry it to the Christians and unbelievers alike. And he said to me: "Tell them, 'I am bringing you news of great joy!' "[2]

This vision convinced Catherine that her local efforts to influence peace, order, and reform — with which she was already involved — must be expanded to reach a wider audience. As a result, she went herself to Avignon, the seat of papal government, where she intervened directly in the international affairs of the Church; she called Pope Gregory XI to his responsibility to bring about reform in Church administration and to return the papal court to Rome. Evoking none of the fearful uncertainty, inner personal struggle, and withdrawal which characterized her reaction to the childhood vision, this mature prayer experience elicited an immediate and purposeful response, one that led her to take authoritative public action. Her mission became universal as she perceived her vocation to be for everyone, Christians and unbelievers, regardless of risk to herself. She chose to suffer the passion of the universal Church in union with Christ, to carry the olive branch of universal peace, and to become a public figure of compassion and mercy, a woman of the Church. Concluding her description of the vision, she was able to describe her call as a public commitment:

> Now what words could ever describe the wonderful things of God? None from this poor wretch! So I'd rather keep silent and give myself completely to seeking God's honor, the salvation of souls, and the renewal and exaltation of holy Church. And by the grace and the power of the Holy Spirit I intend to persevere until I die. [3]

How remarkable is this transformation! What has happened to the hesitant child of six? What secret wisdom and inner discipline has formed the woman of twenty-nine so that she dares to serve the needs of a precarious and violent world, personally taking up the cross of suffering and the olive branch of peace? The explanation lies in the unique spiritual way that Catherine developed during the twenty-three year interval between her two visions, a spirituality revealed in Catherine's own writings, in the pages of her *Letters,* her *Dialogue,* and her *Prayers.*

The ensuing chapters trace the development of Catherine's spiritual life by an examination of a series of significant images which she uses throughout her writings. Superimposing one image on the other, she articulates a spirituality both Trinitarian and Christocentric, one which leads her to seek an interior unity that reflects the mysterious oneness of the Godhead and to embrace the redemptive mission of the Son. Each image highlights a distinctive nuance of progress toward perfection described in the traditional three-staged rhythm of the spiritual life:

withdrawal, interior waiting, and exterior activity; expressed another way, there is an initial accent on the self, then on God, and finally on the neighbor for love of God.

The introductory stage of entrance into self-knowledge to learn humility results in a courageous and anchoring choice to love God and what God loves with an affection and desire that prods her to go forward. In a second stage, an interior transformation occurs that initiates her to the wisdom of God's way, to the secret of the passion of the Son who redeemed her. The third stage accomplishes an outward movement when, fired with God's own charity, an outburst of compassion impels her toward God's people, to a return to activity, to the service of her neighbor. Examining the symbols which disclose the chronology and the dynamic of these stages reveals Catherine's growth from youthful indecision to spiritual maturity, from self-directed enthusiasm to a growing conception of how one loves and serves God, and from personal holiness achieved in solitude to the cosmic sanctity in which loving and serving her neighbor is the only return she can make to the gratuitous love of her God.

ENDNOTES

1. We are dependent on Raymond's *Legenda* for the details of this initial vision. Though Catherine related the story many times, she makes no specific reference to it in the *Dialogue*.
2. *Letters*, 65, pp. 207-208.
3. Ibid., p. 208.

5

IMAGINE A CIRCLE WITH A TREE SPROUTING IN ITS CENTER

When Catherine's family released her from the severe restrictions they had placed upon her freedom to pray, she was able to enter into the quiet of meditation and absorption in God's will where she discovered the foundational importance of self-knowledge. She realized the necessity of growing in personal virtue and of opening herself to the divine gift of discernment. At this point, when she abandoned *admiranda* to embrace more ordinary human means of achieving holiness, Catherine's own version of her spiritual life begins to have meaning. The opening lines of the *Dialogue* state, "She has for some time exercised herself in virtue and has become accustomed to dwelling in the cell of self knowledge." (D. 1:25) Using the common medieval metaphors of "tree" and "light," Catherine demonstrates how virtues develop one from the other and how she opens her understanding to discern the hidden meaning in God's plan for her.

Round and Round within the Circle

Catherine's technique of painting word images in the style of medieval iconography is immediately apparent in the *Dialogue* when she symbolizes the cell of self-knowledge, the central and continuous component of her spiritual way, as a circle of soil outlined in the ground. Here, her tree of life will sprout, grow to maturity, and become fruitful. The circle demonstrates the un-ending nature of self-knowledge which, like the nature of God, "has neither beginning nor end." Catherine specifies, "You can go round and round within this circle, finding neither end nor beginning, yet never leaving the circle." (D. 10:41) One of her prayers indicates the ingredient of the circle which links her to the holy. "I see that you have set us, as it were, in a circle, so that wherever we may go, we are still within this circle" unless we "stumble outside the circle which is the light of most holy faith." (P. 11:89,93)

Within this circle, self-knowledge and knowledge of God interact; one savors and deepens the other. Speaking with God's voice, Catherine states, "But if your knowledge of yourself were isolated from me there would be no full circle at all. Instead, there would be a beginning in self-knowledge, but apart from me it would end in confusion." (D. 10:42) Without integrating the two kinds of knowledge, Catherine will never come to the purpose of her creation, to mirror the image and likeness of God.

In an instruction to her first confessor, Tommaso dalla Fonte, Catherine illustrates this duality by comparing earth and water. Earth represents human self-knowledge. "In the earth we can recognize our own poverty: we see that we are not. For we are not. We see that our being is from God."[1] Then, she continues to explain to Tommaso that knowledge of his own poverty will bring him to knowledge of God, "to the living water, the very core of the knowledge of his true and gentle will which desires nothing but that we be made holy."

She tutors her friend, Alessa dei Saracini, about the neces-sity of the two kinds of knowledge by describing the cell of self-knowledge as two-chambered. "When you are in one, you need to be in the other too," she warns, because "otherwise your soul would fall into either confusion or presumption."[2] Confusion follows concentration on the self; presumption results from at-tending only to God. In the *Dialogue* Catherine adds a description of the circle as two-chambered, a mirrored place wherein she sees both her own reflection and the reflection of God:

> As the soul comes to know herself she also knows God better, for she sees how good he has been to her. In the gentle mirror of God she sees her own dignity: that through no merit of hers but by his creation she is the image of God. (D. 13:48)

In the mirror image of her Creator she sees her own goodness as God's gift; moreover, she also sees the reflection of her unworthiness, the result of her own free choices:

> And in the mirror of God's goodness she sees as well her own unworthiness, the work of her own sin. For just as you can see better the blemish on your face when you look at yourself in a mirror, so the soul who in true self-knowledge rises up with desire to look at herself in the gentle mirror of God with the eye of understanding sees all the more clearly her own defects because of the purity she sees in him. (D. 13:48)

Catherine's use of the mirror symbol, an archetype common in medieval writing,[3] emphasizes imitation and reflection as the interior work which will lead her to perfection. When, within her inner chamber of self-knowledge, her reflection begins to resemble the image of God, she will be approaching the purpose of her creation.

This self-knowledge leads to humility, the food which will nourish Catherine's circle of soil:[4]

> This knowledge of yourself, and of me within yourself, is grounded in the soil of true humility, which is as great as the expanse of the circle (which is knowledge of yourself, united with me, as I have said). (D. 10:41-42)

Humility flourishes when Catherine is able to accept herself as God sees her. "Open your mind's eye and look within me," God states, "and you will see the dignity and beauty of my reasoning creature." (D. 1:26) Her sense of God's love for all creation, and for her in particular, finds expression when Catherine has God say, "It was with providence that I created you, and when I contemplated my creature in myself I fell in love with the beauty of my creation. It pleased me to create you in my image and likeness with great providence." (D. 135:277)

Reflecting the image of the Godhead is Catherine's goal; however, she never loses a sense of the distinction between her humanity and God's divinity. Her statement to God, "You are the One who is," and its corollary, "I am the one who is not," confirms the clarity of this perception. (P. 11:95; 14:123)

The contrast between the perfection of God and Catherine's own reflection in the mirror of God, weakness as well as strength, stimulates her to even deeper humility. Growth in this virtue enables Catherine to look at herself with compassion, to find her worth in the mirror in which she contemplates God, and to move beyond a childlike idea of relationship. In Catherine, this true encounter of a humble human being with the magnitude of God is the beginning of the spiritual life, one which maintains consciousness of both the distance and the immediacy between herself and God.

The circle is the most expressive symbol of Catherine's perception of the rhythmic and continuous nature of spiritual growth, connecting Catherine's spirituality with life, with nature, and with the naturalness of all growing things, like the rings which indicate cycles of growth in the tree trunk. In her circle of soil, where the earth and water, the knowledge of self and God, is nourished by humility and the light of faith, the seed of Catherine's life of virtue awakens. Buried in the dark and silent earth, it breaks free of encumbrance, casts off its protective covering, and throws out roots and a fragile stalk. No longer the child of the vision, Catherine stretches toward maturity, "from darkness . . . into the light of true knowledge." (D. 7:36) Drawn to the full extent of her human reason — enlightened by the baptismal gift of faith — Catherine is spurred to a desire that will energize her for the remainder of her life.

A Tree Made for Love

With her new-found wisdom, knowing herself, her nature, and God's love more clearly, Catherine turns from imitation of the heroic sanctity of the *Golden Legends*. She understands that the major task facing beginners is to build a foundation of ordinary virtue. In the first petition of the four in the *Dialogue*, she indicates its primary importance:

> [S]he knew that she could be of no service to her neighbors in teaching or example or prayer without first doing herself the service of attaining and possessing virtue. (D. 1:26)

So, she makes a free choice to follow the way of virtue, a choice that she symbolizes as entering into a thorn bush:

> Beforehand, this decision is a thorn bush they seem to encounter when they follow the way of truth . . . as soon as they decide courageously, despising themselves, and say, "I want to follow Christ crucified," the thorn bush is broken and they discover my immeasurable tenderness, as I showed you at that time.[5] (D. 44:90)

Writing to Archbishop da Itri, Catherine refers to the thorn symbolism. "I wish there were no temptations or illusions of the devil planted like thorns to block our way," she declares. Then, reflecting her own experience of decisiveness, she adds "once they have seen themselves and discovered God's goodness. . . . For nothing would they choose to turn back."[6]

The nature of thorns testifies to the kind of suffering involved in Catherine's early choices since thorns scratch and inflict surface wounds but seldom penetrate deeply into the flesh. In the beginning of a spiritual life, suffering stems from immaturity and reflects ordinary human anxiety in one's desire to achieve a higher level of being. In her early struggle to identify the proper path, Catherine exhibited these emotions, indicative of self-love and self-will. Doubt and uncertainty, urgency and impatience, fear and anger surfaced when her will was thwarted. In itself, futile, ineffectual, and self-imposed, this kind of suffering is, nevertheless, an essential stage of growth. Once it leads to proper choices, made with attentive thought and prayerful consideration, it results in wisdom and purification from sin and selfishness. [7] Catherine confirms that she is growing in this understanding when she makes the distinction that "the value is not in the suffering but in the soul's desire." (D. 4:29)

When she describes the process of growing in virtue, Catherine word-paints the archetypal symbol of the tree with a facile brush that imprints a more gracious image than the spare awkward diagrams found in medieval texts. [8] The creative flow of her imagination and her practical knowledge of husbandry combine to evoke instead the image of a tree like those native to her Tuscan landscape, a tree vibrating with life-giving juices and marrow, a tree that develops through stages from a minuscule seed to the fullness of its growth: roots, stem, branches, buds, flowers, and fruit. Her word-pictures detail the nourishing requisites for her sapling to grow, to endure, and to perform its appropriate task: to produce flowers of virtue and fruits of action. [9] That the tree represents herself, love the purpose of her life, and God the source of that love becomes clear when she states: "Think of the soul as a tree made for love and living only by love. Indeed, without this divine love, which is true and perfect charity, death would be her fruit instead of life." (D. 10:41)

Catherine continually emphasizes the importance of the circle of soil to the nature of the tree that will develop. For example, when she says, "Imagine a circle traced on the ground, and in its center a tree sprouting," she continues:

> The tree finds its nourishment in the soil within the expanse of the circle, but uprooted from the soil it would die fruitless. . . . The circle in which this tree's root, the soul's love, must grow is true knowledge of herself, knowledge that is joined to me, who like the circle have neither beginning nor end. (D. 10:41)

Therefore, it is the nourishment of the roots which first concerns Catherine. "What gives life to both the tree and its branches is its root," she declares, "so long as that root is planted in the soil of humility." (D. 9:40) Consistently, Catherine juxtaposes humility and pride, declaring that the tree of virtue is "put down in the valley of humility" while the tree of death is "planted on the mountain of pride." (D. 4:29; 31:73) Humility fosters life, virtue, and love; pride robs the soul of life, fills it with self-love, and kills virtue. Pride is a worm of self-love gnawing away at the root of the tree, threatening its life; "it cripples the root of our tree so that it can produce no fruit of life. The tree withers and its fruits dry up, and its freshness does not last."[10]

Catherine's letters to Pope Gregory XI reveal this contrast. She declares, "I want you to be a tree of love . . . a tree with its roots in deep humility, for God's honor and the salvation of your little sheep."[11] Then, addressing the problem of pride and self-love, the opposite of humility, Catherine expresses a vehemence equal to the importance of the person she is addressing:

> For those who love themselves — whether they are rulers or the ruled — harbor within themselves the evil pride that is the head and origin of all evil. For those who are isolated in their self-centeredness, loving themselves selfishly and not for God, can do nothing but evil; all virtue is dead in them.[12]

Pride and self-love, then, are "the principle and foundation of evil" (D. 7:35) because they kill the life of charity without which "no virtue can have life in it." (D. 4:29) Charity is the virtue essential to the tree structure, but its vitality is dependent on the degree of humility produced in the circle of soil. As long as the tree is rooted in the soil of humility, charity will flourish, Catherine declares, because "humility is the governess and wet nurse of charity" (D. 9:40), it "nurses and mothers" charity to life. (D. 4:29)

Interdependence is essential in the virtuous life. Nourished by humility, charity, in turn, "gives life to all the virtues"; (D. 7:36) it "has many offshoots, like a tree with many branches." (D. 9:40) For Catherine, charity is so joined to patience, "that the one cannot live without the other." (D. 5:33) Patience is the marrow of the tree of virtue, the life-sustaining element which must penetrate to every branch and twig of the tree structure if it is to flourish. Just as the absence of interior marrow in a tree becomes manifest to observers by its exterior dead leaves and branches, so too a deficiency in patience in Catherine's exterior demeanor will indicate the lack of divine charity within her. God says that patience is "a sure sign that I am in her and that she is united with me." (D. 10:42)

A tree with a healthy marrow will bear a fruitful crown; blossoms will bud, flower, and produce fruit. Similarly, in Catherine's tree of virtue, when humility nourishes charity and charity kindles patience, all the virtues blossom. The fruits which they produce, acts of charity performed in loving response to the need of her neighbor, benefit both Catherine and the recipients of her charity:

> This tree so delightfully planted, bears many-fragranced blossoms of virtue. Its fruit is grace for the soul herself and blessings for her neighbors in proportion to the conscientiousness of those who would share my servants' fruits. (D. 10:42)

The tree of virtue symbolizes Catherine's life work, developing and exercising a rhythmic progression of virtues — one enabling the other — until virtue becomes so impregnated in her that she can blossom and bear fruit in an active ministry. A young tree is earthbound, unable to care for anything beyond its own survival, but a mature tree stretches far into the heavens to give rest and comfort to the birds of the air. Similarly, Catherine, in the beginning, concerned with the roots and nourishment of her life-tree, knew little of the tree's crown looming far beyond her vision. However, maturing to full growth, she did what she was created to do, yielding "the fragrance of glory and praise" to God. (D. 10:42) Symbolizing her creaturehood in the face of divinity, the crown — "the divine nature joined to the earth of your humanity" — blossoms in patience, courage, and perseverance. When these virtues are strong, Catherine says, nothing can hurt her; she will be "patient and strong in suffering, and persevering." (D. 44:90; 77:141-142)

A Shoot Grafted into Its Side

As a graphic image, the tree of virtue is a self-evident metaphor of Catherine's life; it is, perhaps, the most concrete of her symbols. Its three parts clearly interconnect with one another, grow one from the other, then flourish together as one unit, clearly typifying how the three stages of spiritual growth interact throughout her life. Understanding this symbol, with its stages of preparation, interior development, and exterior concern for her neighbor, lays a firm foundation for further interpretation for Catherine will continually superimpose new images on this basic one as an artist adds color and tone to a painting to heighten meaning and enhance its message. With each addition, her symbolism becomes increasingly abstract.

When Catherine introduces the concept of discernment as a

graft on her tree, she implies that it has a character that is more than human. When she equates discernment with "light," a traditional figure of growth in understanding,[13] Catherine suggests that comprehension of God's intention for her develops with the light of grace and faith. In addition, she states that discernment uniquely affects the quality of her virtue and her activity:

> Discernment is that light which dissolves all darkness, dissipates ignorance, and seasons every virtue and virtuous deed. It has a prudence that cannot be deceived, a strength that is invincible, a constancy right up to the end, reaching as it does from heaven to earth, that is, from the knowledge of me to the knowledge of oneself, from love of me to love of one's neighbors. (D. 11:44-45)

Thus, discernment, grafted into the tree, seasons the marrow of patience and charity already nourished by the humility yielded in the circle of knowledge of self and of God. The two are "engrafted together and planted in the soil of that true humility which is born of self-knowledge." (D. 9:41) Like the tree itself, "only when discernment is rooted in humility is it virtuous"; only then, Catherine says, is it capable of "producing life-giving fruit and willingly yielding what is due to everyone." (D. 9:40)

The purpose of grafting, a procedure familiar in Catherine's Tuscan countryside, is to combine the unique qualities of two different species to create one where quality surpasses either of the originals. In Catherine's case, the graft of discernment changes forever the nature of her life, virtue, and action. As discernment enters into the tree of virtue to alter forever its nature, so too the divine light of grace enters into the darkness of Catherine's mind to change her way of perceiving. She becomes a different person, one whose vision gradually enlarges to encompass God's will and the need of her neighbor.

Catherine symbolizes her growth in discernment as moving through three lights of understanding. In the *Dialogue,* she characterizes the first light as the way of ordinary virtue and love, where she discerns with natural human reason and with ordinary understanding. This "is the ordinary light," she says, "and everyone must have it." (D. 98:184-185) In this light, she comes to recognize the transitory nature of human and material things and to make choices based on this understanding. She makes it clear, however, that even this ordinary light of reason is drawn from God, the "true Light," and is exercised through "the eye of understanding" with the baptismal "gift of faith":

> If you exercise this faith by virtue with the light of reason, reason will in turn be enlightened by faith, and such faith will give you life and lead you in the way of truth. With this light you will reach me, the true Light; without it you would come to darkness. (D. 98:185)

Writing to Iacopo da Itri, about the requisites for entering the beginning stage of the spiritual life, Catherine speaks of Christ as the light. Knowing his goodness, she writes, one must "open the eye of their understanding and reason to see" and having seen, run on to follow Christ attentively and eagerly, without stopping to look back, because they are so caught up in "their will and desire to follow Christ."[14] The will, she tells da Itri, is a strong hand that holds the two-edged sword of hatred and love, "the contempt I have conceived for sin, and the love I have conceived for virtue."[15]

Desire grows in the first light of reason. Catherine emphasizes its necessity in a letter to her friend Bartolomeo urging, "Lose yourself completely, with insatiable desire."[16] Desire enables her to follow the guiding principle of the first light, always to choose good over evil, loving what God loves and hating what God hates. The desire enkindled in the first light must remain operative throughout the entire spiritual life because there will be regression rather than progress if affection and desire fade.

Catherine's constant prayer is to stand firm in holy desire and continue to grow in it. (P. 16:143)

Continually making free choices to love what God loves — virtue — by turning away from the opposite — vice — requires the consistent exercise of love and desire. These free decisions and choices confirm Catherine's path in life and lead her from adolescence to maturity. The guiding principle, to love what God loves and hate what God hates, expresses her perception that vice will be eradicated by the practice of virtue and that a constant choosing to love virtue will prove and strengthen her hatred of vice. (D. 98:185) She tells a wavering priest to "Fall in love with true virtue; its effect is the opposite of the vice."[17]

Many of Catherine's discoveries in the first light restore calm to her spirit and help her to attune herself to the pace of nature with its rhythmic, gradual, and orderly progression. The urgency and anxiety that led her to seek instant sanctity diminish as she grows in the humility which enables relationship. Progressing beyond the first light, however, requires that Catherine relinquish control and permit God to choose what is best for her. Only in this way, by this act of faith, can she proceed to greater perfection.

In the second light, a time of deepening discernment, purification is the dynamic of growth. Catherine's spirit is tested; she is provided opportunity to strengthen virtue, to temper self-will, and to deepen knowledge of herself and God, a knowledge "more perfectly gained in time of temptation." (D. 43:88) Experience teaches Catherine that God provides whatever is required to bring her to great perfection. (D. 68:130) Discovering that consolation, though comforting, is not essential to love, Catherine learns to rest in God's providential care, to reverence consolation and trials as equal gifts of a loving God. This transforming understanding marks Catherine's passage from loving what God loves to the guiding principle of the second light, accepting with reverence whatever God sends her. (D. 99:187)

Courage and steadfastness grow as Catherine waits on God in faith with humility, patience, and love. (D. 95:117) She develops the virtue of prudence which leads her to understand that the holiness she sought to achieve by asceticism is, in reality, a pure gift given only at God's will and pleasure. It becomes clear to her that it is not "beating down the body" that will bring her to perfection, but conquering self-will; God must be allowed to name "the time, the place, and the situation" of her life. (D. 99:186-187) Catherine will be led in the way of perfection when she is "immersed in and subject to" the gentle will of God which will teach her the "gentle straight way" marked out by Christ's own suffering. (D. 104:197) What God requires, she learns, is not just "infinite desire," but a will in harmony with the divine will. Therefore, by choosing the way of the second light, Catherine accepts with reverence whatever God sends. (D. 100:188)

Like the marrow of the tree trunk, discernment permeates Catherine's whole being in the second light. Realizing that patience and suffering go hand in hand and that true suffering accepts anything at all that God gives, she abandons her own narrow vision of penance. (D. 5:33) "Everything comes from me," God says, "not a leaf falls from a tree apart from my providence," and "I give and permit what I do" to accomplish your sanctification. (D. 60:114) She shares this wisdom with a woman who lives in fear for the safety of her family. "Not a leaf falls from a tree" without God's consent, Catherine writes. "So, not only should you not fear this thing — because God gives us what we can bear and no more — but let's accept it with reverence. . . ." Allowing God to choose for her, trusting that everything God does "is for love," accepting "everything with love and reverence,"[18] leads Catherine beyond the second light of acceptance to the way of greatest perfection: willing what God chooses for her and seeking only God's honor and the salvation of souls. (D. 104:197)

To will what God wills is the guiding principle of the third light. What it entails is clear as God declares, "I prune you by means of trials: disgrace, insults, mockery, abuse, and reproach, . . . with hunger and thirst, by words and actions, as it pleases my goodness to grant to each of you as you are able to endure." (D. 145:303) In this light of discernment, the virtue of patience grows so strong that Catherine relishes opportunities to love those who do not love her, and patience in suffering leads her to compassion for others. Just as the outstretched branches of the tree bear buds, blossoms, and fruits strong enough to endure the vagaries of weather and to survive and prosper, so Catherine, too, will flourish in the midst of opposition and conflict.

"If you are a tree of love so sweetly rooted, you will find the fruit of patience and strength at the tips of your branches, and crowned perseverance nested within you," she promised Pope Gregory XI. "You will find peace and quiet and consolation in suffering when you see yourself conformed in that suffering with Christ crucified."[19] Catherine wrote to the prior of a monastery outside of Genoa about the burning love of Christ which often acts as medicine for the soul. Listing the "bitter things" that are part of life, "all sorts of darkness, temptation, spiritual frustration, or other troubles that come from outside ourselves," she encourages him that they will give birth in him to "justice, and a holy gentle patience" by which he will be able "to endure any pain and torment," and consider himself undeserving of "spiritual peace and quiet."[20] It is this same medicine that purifies Catherine's love in the third light. Because she wills what God wills, God's own compassionate love overflows in Catherine's heart, impelling her to go out, to share God's love for humanity, and make it known to the world.[21] This interior transformation will manifest itself publicly just as the tree of virtue is visibly fruitful when the marrow of patience is flowing freely throughout the tree.

However, Catherine came only gradually to this commitment to others. When she reached eighteen, her family consented to her becoming a Mantellate and, though her life continued to be solitary, she began, in Raymond's words, to live a serious religious life. To the ordinary requirements of the rule of the Mantellate — obedience to superiors, daily prayer, penance, and acts of charity — she added personal vows whereby she espoused the evangelical counsels of poverty, chastity, and obedience as well as a vow of silence with everyone except her confessor, the Dominican family friend Tommaso dalla Fonte.

Her only contact with the public came as she made her way to and from the Church of San Domenico each day, but as she progressed in self-knowledge, in the exercise of virtue, and in the ability to choose to love what God loved, she came to a more mature understanding of her role in the work of redemption. Slowly emerging from solitude, Catherine first tended to the domestic affairs of her own family with characteristic vigor and intensity. Soon, her charity extended beyond her own household in corporal and spiritual works of mercy; with her father's permission, she began to distribute the goods of the family to the poor. (L. 118-119) Her personal attention to the needy and infirm dates from this period. Raymond recounted incidents concerning older women, usually Mantellate, whom Catherine tended despite repulsive physical circumstances, and in some cases, in an atmosphere of severe animosity and jealousy. (L. 140-146)

Gradually growing in the wisdom of discernment, Catherine's works of charity expanded and her reputation grew. She began to attract followers: men and women, lay and religious. Some were preachers, educated in theology and philosophy; others were poets and painters. [22] Conversation with them about theological questions and the political and social issues of the day nourished and stretched her mind. She became aware and informed about current religious and political issues; the papal residence in Avignon and its effect on violence, lawlessness, and civic discord in all of Italy; the decadent state of the lives of clerics serving the Church which was visible in high ranking clergy no less than in the lower orders; local issues of family wars, violence, and vendettas. Catherine brought back each of these issues into her solitude, her prayer, and her intense absorption in God.

Thus, discernment, developing integrally with all the virtues, fostered or "seasoned" Catherine's spiritual life. The "light" of Christ guarded her from too great a concentration on herself so that, living in the third light, she could be "peaceful and calm," permitting nothing to scandalize her. She could "stand in the water of great troubles and temptations" in peace. (D. 100:189)

ENDNOTES

1. *Letters*, 3, p. 44.
2. *I, Catherine*, Letter 33, p. 151.
3. Some titles of spiritual literature, contemporaneous with Catherine and familiar to her, which utilized the device of the mirror include: *Specchio della Croce* (The Mirror of the Cross) by the Dominican Domenico Cavalca (1270-1342) and *Specchio di vera penitenza* (The Mirror of True Penitence) by Jacopo Passavanti (c. 1300-1357).
4. Two centuries later Teresa of Avila illustrated the spiritual life as seven mansions through which she made her way to union with God in the innermost room. Teresa told her sisters, "self-knowledge is so important that, even if you were raised right up to the heavens, I should like you never to relax your cultivation of it." She, too, associated self-knowledge with the cultivation of humility; she recommended beginning "by entering the room where humility is acquired." *The Complete Works of Saint Teresa of Jesus*, 2 vol., tr. and ed. by E. Allison Peers, New York, Sheed and Ward, 1946; *Interior Castle*, II, pp. 203, 208.
5. When Catherine was ten, her sister Bonaventura prevailed upon her to submit to some of the local courting customs, such as washing her neck, bleaching her hair, and making herself visible in the doorway. In the midst of these preparations, Bonaventura died while giving birth; immediately, Catherine renewed her determination to lead a solitary, celibate, and consecrated life. (L. 36-38) Her slight wavering from her promise of virginity, in submitting to Bonaventura's enticements, remained a painful memory; years later, in the *Dialogue* she likened this experience to a "thorn bush" encountered as one approached the "tree of virtue."
6. *Letters*, 56, p. 175.
7. In a taped lecture, "Conscious Labor and Intentional Suffering," J.G. Bennett details how one grows from self-concerned effort to the purity of "intentional suffering" for the good of humanity. *Commentaries on Beelzebub's Tales*, Shelbourne House Talk 24, Claymont Communications, Charles Town, West Virginia, 1981.
8. See, for example, the twelfth century diagram of the tree of virtue based on the writings of Gregory the Great. The base was humility; branches of virtue extended

out: Justice, Prudence, Temperance, Fortitude, Faith, and Hope, all presided over by Charity. Extensions, or applications of the virtues, flowed out from each like blossoms. Meiss, fig. 162.

9. Bennett declares that a human, like Catherine's firmly rooted tree, is also driven by his/her own nature to grow and to achieve a life purpose. Ibid.

10. *Letters*, 54, p. 166.

11. Ibid., 88, p. 266.

12. Ibid., 54, p. 166.

13. A recent dissertation, from the perspective of theology, presented a textual study of discernment seen through Catherine's images of "lights." See Diana Villegas, "A Comparison of Catherine of Siena's and Ignatius of Loyola's Teaching on Discernment," University Microfilms, Inc., Michigan, 1987 (Fordham University, New York, 1986). For the purpose of this monograph, the three lights will be analyzed in terms of content, or process of growth in the individual. In the *Dialogue*, God instructed Catherine in the three lights as a method of evaluating progress in souls, for the purpose of spiritual direction.

14. *Letters*, 56, 175-176.

15. Ibid.

16. Ibid., 4, p. 46.

17. Ibid., 10, p. 58.

18. Ibid., 12, pp. 61-62.

19. Ibid., 88, p. 266.

20. Ibid., 85, p. 256.

21. Bennett labels this kind of suffering intentional, the suffering in which one chooses to do for another regardless of the fact that personal hardship is involved. Ibid.

22. It was at this time that Catherine met the young Dominican, Bartolomeo Dominici, who was an unofficial counselor in the troubled years before Raymond of Capua was officially assigned as Catherine's confessor. He was well-educated, a scholar, and supportive of her tenuous position within the Sienese Dominican family.

6

CHRIST HAS MADE A STAIRCASE
OF HIS BODY

Catherine's words range freely over her canvas to portray the tree of virtue. Soil and roots, trunk and marrow, blossoming crown — each with its symbolic content — stand revealed. So does the graft of discernment which permeates the tree's marrow to season all its growth. As Catherine grows in virtue and in her ability to comprehend meaning and purpose in God's plan for her, she begins to articulate spiritual progress in more complex mystical language. She merges two metaphors whereby her tree of virtue becomes the tree of the cross. The roots are the feet of the crucified; the marrow enclosed within is the heart of the divine victim; and the expansive and fruitful crown is the mouth of Christ. The body of Christ crucified is "hollowed out" with three stairs which in turn are the three stages of perfection. This Christocentric imagery then assumes a Trinitarian formulation as Catherine declares that the stairs or stages are synonymous with her three human powers: the memory, the understanding, and the will. When these powers are unified in a harmonious reflection of the three in one of the three persons in the Godhead, Catherine will come to unity with the Godhead. She will mirror the image of the Trinity.

Climbing the Tree of the Holy Cross

In a letter to a group of cloistered religious women, Catherine makes explicit reference to the symbolism of the feet, heart, and mouth of Christ crucified, stating, "To make it possible for us to climb to this perfection, Christ has actually made a staircase of his body."[1] Furthermore, she conveys to the prior of a monastery in the outskirts of Siena an explicit parallel between the two tree images by using the biblical story of Zacchaeus who, being very short, climbed the sycamore tree to get a better view of Christ.[2] Equating smallness of stature with "hearts that are narrow" and "low in charity," she advises the prior to "do the same as Zacchaeus." Then, connecting at once to the deeper image, she immediately abandons the sycamore tree and embraces the metaphor of the tree of the cross. She writes, "Let us climb the tree of the most holy cross," to see and touch God and "find the fire of his inestimable charity." And she explains how one can make this climb:

> And if you say: "I can't climb this tree; it's too high," I answer that he has hollowed out steps for you in his body. First, raise yourself, heart and soul, to the feet of God's Son; then climb up to the heart, which is open and utterly spent for us, and so arrive at the peace of his mouth where you will learn to savour souls and make them your food, and in this way become a true shepherd ready to lay down your life for your sheep.[3]

Christ's nailed feet, like the roots of the tree, provide anchor and refuge for the beginner. The pierced heart, hidden and pulsing with life like the marrow of the tree trunk, nourishes and sustains the life of the spirit. The open parched mouth through which Catherine enters into Christ, like the crown of the tree, symbolizes her fruitfulness for others and the universal redemptive purpose of her life. Climbing the symbolic stairs, Catherine

develops interiorly for she adds, "You will recognize in these three stairs three spiritual stages." (D. 26:64)

Describing Christ's feet, Catherine observes that they are nailed fast to the cross to form the first stair, a condition she associates with the giving up of self-will so that one develops a "deep and genuine humility."[4] The analogy between the nailed feet and the roots of the tree securely bound by the soil is sharpened by this reference to humility, the essential ingredient of the soil of virtue. Catherine extends the parallel when she states, "we can never have any virtue at all if we don't climb the first stair."[5]

When she steps up to the feet of Christ, Catherine's love is still imperfect. She calls it the "love of pleasure and self-advantage" because, in God, she has found "both pleasure and profit." (D. 63:118) Moreover, she says, many take this "common stair" out of fear and weariness; however, if they persevere and take advantage of the light of discernment, they may begin to progress to love of virtue. At the first stair, love must become strong enough to cast out fear and overcome weariness; this is the area where change must take place because love is essential to growth in virtue. (D. 49:100-101)

To demonstrate this change that is taking place within her, Catherine speaks of her own feet as well as those of Christ crucified. She says that affection must motivate the one who takes her first step up to the nailed feet of Christ crucified for, "just as the feet carry the body, the affections carry the soul."[6] (D. 26:64) With growing discernment, however, she declares that the first ordinary step must be climbed "with both feet — that is, with affection and desire." (D. 49:100-101) Increasing desire overcomes fear and purifies Catherine's love; she realizes that she is not alone, not dependent solely on her own effort. Instead, she learns to rely on God's mercy. Choosing to love what God loves, she discovers the greatness of God's love for her and is moved to a loving dependence on God.

Catherine's increased desire, her love of virtue, and the growing clarity of her discernment lead her to the realization that what is significant is her free will. Thus, freely choosing to love as God loves, she opts to advance to a higher level of perfection. The courage to do this results from the tremendous desire and unquenchable thirst that is the fruit of the first step of affection and will. Catherine does what she advises others to do. "Climb the next stair without delay," she advises, "and you come to the open side of God's Son. There you will find the fiery abyss of divine charity."[7] Catherine says, "Only hearts as hard as diamonds could fail to be softened by such measureless love."[8]

Christ's open wounded heart, the symbol of the second stair, is rich in power to convey the wealth of love Catherine finds there:

> At this second stair, his open side, you find a shop filled with fragrant spices. There you find the God-Man. There your soul is so sated and drunk that you lose all self-consciousness, just like a drunkard intoxicated with wine; you see nothing but his blood, shed with such blazing love.[9]

At Christ's heart, Catherine "exercises love" and receives "the fruit" of God's goodness. (D. 95:177) Hidden within the open heart of Christ, her development is analogous to the interior marrow of the tree of virtue. Catherine's work is to wait while God's work is to produce fruit in her. As she wrote to Tommaso dalla Fonte, "we enter that flaming, consumed heart, opened up like a window without shutters, never to be closed," where with the free will given by God, "we see and we know that his will has become nothing but our sanctification."[10]

As Catherine comes "to know . . . the power of the blood," she becomes one with Christ's passion. (D. 75:137-138) An interior infused wisdom leads her to open herself to the suffering, pain, and powerlessness of which the heart — open, wounded, and bleeding — speaks. Suffering at the second stair comes from deep within herself and the dark side of Catherine's personality becomes apparent to her. The high opinion that she had of her love and spirit of sacrifice gives way before the realization that she has enjoyed determining her own way in the spiritual life and that her love of God is bound up in her own pleasure.

Thus exposed to the fragility of her human capability to love and having realized the totality of giving which true love implies, Catherine turns in humble acceptance to God who alone can teach her so great a love. Reminding her that suffering is the way of the Son, God instructs her to learn the love of the passion. "I made him a bridge for you," and now, "no one can come to me except through him." (D. 53:106) Suffering purifies and transforms her spirit; it opens her inner being to God at work within her. Bearing pain and suffering which she has not chosen for herself with patience and humility leads her to a different and higher level of being. [11]

At Christ's side, Catherine receives the wisdom to know "the secret of his heart" and the grace of "being joined and kneaded into the blood." (D. 75:138) Loving what God loves grows to a loving acceptance of the divine providence of God in the good and bad things that happen in her life. As she begins to love with the love that inspired Christ to endure the passion, Catherine "experiences and absorbs such a burning love that she runs on to the third stair" where "it is clear that she has arrived at perfection." (D. 76:140)

Catherine's ascent to the third stair, the mouth of Christ crucified, symbolizes her entry into union with God to become absorbed into the flesh and blood of divinity like food. The mouth, therefore, is a symbol overflowing with meaning. At one level, conscious of the liturgical kiss of peace, Catherine says that she enters into a sea of peace where she "finds such a peace that there is nothing that can disturb her. She has let go of and drowned her own will, and when that will is dead there is peace and quiet." (D. 76:141) At the mouth of Christ, "you find rest in quiet calm; there you taste the peace of obedience," she explains as she continues her metaphor of one drunk with love:

> A person who is really completely drunk, good and full, falls asleep, and in that sleep feels neither pleasure nor pain. So, too, the spouse of Christ, sated with love, falls asleep in the peace of her Bridegroom. Her feelings too are asleep so that, even if all sorts of trouble befall her, they don't disturb her at all. [12]

The peace found at Christ's mouth is of such depth that it cannot be ruffled by exterior conflict for there Catherine is "conformed with Christ crucified, united with him." [13] She has completed what "he has asked me so often — to live as dead to my perverse will." [14]

Developing the symbolism of the mouth as the means of serving her neighbor, Catherine speaks of two languages spoken with "the tongue of holy and constant prayer." Interiorly, she offers "tender loving desires for the salvation of souls"; exteriorly, she uses the language by which she will carry out her public ministry, "admonishing, advising, testifying, without any fear for the pain the world may please to inflict on her." (D. 76:140) The one tongue speaking two languages represents the integration of contemplation and action by which every time and place becomes for Catherine a time and place for prayer. (D. 74:137) Activity for her neighbor is prayer, and silent contemplation before God produces blessings for her neighbor. Like the swell and the trough of the ocean's surface, each is one with the other.

Consequently, at the third stair, Catherine's emphasis shifts from her relationship with God to its manifestation through her neighbor, the exercise of a public ministry. The tribulations which begin to assail her only deepen her inner calm. Transformed in the fire of the Spirit's mercy, she is filled with a compassion for others in which the virtue of patience comes to perfection. With it, Catherine is ready to be fruitful for her neighbor despite the sufferings which come unbidden as anger, envy, and jealousy surround her, and resentment flares among her townspeople. The dedication and deference accorded her by the growing numbers of followers fuel an atmosphere of conflict centering on her eating habits, her public displays of ecstasy, and the growing demand for her presence outside of Siena.

When Catherine's abstinence from food became the subject of public gossip, the reaction of some included amazement and wonder; others saw her eating habits in a less favorable light. Some called it a trick of the devil while others charged her with outright deceit; the last of these accused her of pretending to fast while eating sumptuously in secret. (L. 159) Her opponents lodged complaints with her confessor, Tommaso dalla Fonte. Unsure about what to do, Tommaso reprimanded Catherine, told her that her visions came from the devil, and ordered her to eat. [15] (L. 153-154) Obediently complying as best she could, Catherine suffered in the process. Like other holy women of the medieval period, she had engaged in early practices of extreme self-denial with food which permanently affected her ability to eat with any degree of normality. [16]

Equal attention was focused on Catherine's ecstatic behavior in public, usually when she received the Eucharist in the Church of San Domenico. Catherine's emotional response to this experience, which she likened to the total immersion whereby the fish is in the sea and the sea is in the fish, left her numb and seemingly paralyzed and exposed to inquisitive stares for a period of hours. (D. 112:211) By some, she was considered to be a nuisance and a source of scandal; she was ordered to control her emotions and cease her sobs and devotional noises. (L. 170, 290) She was forbidden to stay in the church, lest she delay those who wished to close it up; the extreme among her critics lifted her up bodily, carried her outside the church, and left her on the ground; the malicious, doubting her, kicked her or pricked her body with needles. (L. 287, 365) Tommaso, once again deluged with complaints about his penitent, reluctantly acceded to the critics and limited Catherine's freedom to receive the Eucharist. He required her to request communion only with his express permission and only from his hands. Catherine experienced intense suffering from this deprivation; however, she also received abundant consolation when God intervened directly to assuage her grief. In the *Dialogue* she recounts several of these instances in detail. [17] (L. 171)

The third area of contention — Catherine's increasing notoriety both within and without Siena — was the direct result of the tendency of medieval people to be drawn toward holy persons. [18] She became an object of intense interest, not only among the simple and unlettered, but among the intellectual and the mighty. "The virgin's fame began to spread abroad, until it finally reached the Apostolic throne and the ears of most of the Cardinals," reported Raymond. (L. 370) Requests for her intervention in public and private matters multiplied as her reputation for sanctity spread.

Letters from this early period document Catherine's contacts with influential individuals involved in public affairs. When Cardinal Iacopo Orsini, the "official 'protector' of the Sienese Republic at the papal court in Avignon" passed through Siena in 1371, he met Catherine personally. In a letter during 1374, she urges him to use his influence to expedite her three enduring wishes: the return of the Pope to Italy, the calling of a crusade, and an end to internal warfare among Christians. [19] A letter to Bartolomeo Dominici in Pisa conveys the information that Pope Gregory XI has sent a representative to Siena to request her "special prayer for him and for the Church." [20] Catherine, in turn, sent the pope a personal message requesting that she and her followers be allowed to offer their bodies as sacrifice in a crusade. [21]

A personal reference to the conflicts surrounding her appears in a letter to Piero Gambacorta, the ruler of Pisa, in which

Catherine alludes to his invitation to visit that city. Citing first her poor physical condition, she also states that her visit might be a source of scandal — relations between Pisa and Siena being strained at the time. Finally, she suggests other problems:

> But I trust in God's goodness, that if he sees that it is for his honor and the salvation of souls, he will see that I come free of constraint, in peace, and without any further gossip. [22]

Raymond refers more directly to the situation among the Sienese Dominicans. Attention directed to Catherine, one of the youngest of the Sienese Mantellate, caused older members to seek to restrain her freedom. Catherine was confronted by "superiors and others who tried to stop her from going certain places where by divine revelation she had been ordered to go and from doing things that the Lord had commanded her to do." (L. 363) Raymond spoke of "tactless superiors, of priors who hadn't the faintest idea what they were doing, all of whom kept trying to stop Catherine from going to confession and communion and from performing all the other acts to which her piety prompted her." (L. 364) Torn between obedience to those who represented authority and obedience to directives which she felt came from divine authority, Catherine was harassed by the Sisters of Penance, who said "evil things about the way she was behaving in public and in private" and convinced the "superiors of the Order" that her works were of the devil and that she should be reprimanded. (L. 365) Their attempts to terminate her membership in the Sisters of Saint Dominic placed both her person and her reputation in jeopardy. [23]

All of these situations give Catherine ample opportunities to grow in virtue and to demonstrate the depth of her dedication to her neighbor. The same intensity and ardor which previously characterized her pursuit of personal perfection now marks Catherine's public career. Loving God and loving her neighbor have become one and the same thing; loving and serving her neighbor is the only means that she has to return God's love for her. At the peak of spiritual development, Catherine turns with all the love of her being to the service of her neighbor. She can respond to the encompassing love which God showers upon her in no other way. Catherine has reached a mature spirituality and she is prepared to be a significant worker in the garden of God's Church.

Gathered, United, Immersed, and Set Afire

Catherine's symbolic tree of virtue is now one with the tree of the cross; mingling the marrow of patience and the seasoning of discernment with Christ's own redemptive blood has united her own search for perfection to Christ's sacrificial mission of redemption. Catherine's life belongs to God's Church and God's people. What remains, however, is her explanation of how she comes to mirror the unity of the Trinity. To do this she goes deep within her own self to find the image of the Godhead and the means to mirror that sacred image. Looking within her human self and within the Godhead, she discovers in each a triple essence: in herself, three reasoning powers of memory, understanding, and will; in the Godhead, three distinct persons, the Father, the Son, and the Spirit.

Just as each of the divine persons had a specific role in the creation, redemption, and sanctification of humanity, so too does Catherine see that each of her three human powers contributes uniquely to her sanctification.[24] She reasons that the development of each one to its utmost potential and the functioning together of all three in unified harmony, one helping the other, will bring her to an interior integration that will image the unity and harmony of the Trinitarian Godhead. Thus, Catherine will achieve her goal of coming to the image and likeness of the God who created her.

In this prayer from the *Dialogue*, Catherine portrays her sense of the bonding that exists between the persons of the divine Trinity and her own powers of memory, understanding, and will:

> You, Eternal Father, gave us memory to hold your gifts and share your power. You gave us understanding so that, seeing your goodness, we might share the wisdom of your only-begotten Son. And you gave us free will to love what our understanding sees and knows of your truth, and so share the mercy of your Holy Spirit. (D. 13:49)

Catherine's connection between the divine attributes and the operation of the reasoning powers is consistent with the knowledge that the memory stores ideas, impulses, affections, emotions, imaginative events, and bits of conversation which can pour out in undisciplined streams from the unconscious. Surveying this data, the understanding identifies what is true and useful while the will chooses whether or not to act upon what the understanding perceives. If the will, with its freedom to embrace what it loves, chooses to actualize what the memory has surfaced and what the understanding has recognized, the three powers fuse as one unit, act in harmony, and achieve a conscious result. [25]

Catherine interprets this rational activity of the three powers as a rhythmic reflection of the interaction of the divine Trinity. Corresponding to the creative power of the Father, the memory initiates remembrances of God's benevolence; the understanding, paralleling the wisdom of the Son, acknowledges these memories and redeems them from the unconscious. The will, like the merciful and sanctifying love of the Spirit, chooses to bring to realization what the memory and the understanding have made conscious. Then, fused as in a physical fire, the three powers become one harmonious unit to reflect the Godhead. (D. 4:32; 119:222)

Describing this interaction to Cardinal de Luna, Catherine writes, "Let your memory be filled with this precious Blood; let your understanding see and comprehend the wisdom of the Word, God's only-begotten Son, . . . And let your will, as if inebriated with the blood of Christ . . . make all haste to love, loving him with heart, soul, and strength until death, with no thought for self but only for Christ crucified. . . ."[26] The pre-eminent role of free will in this process, and the unity that it fosters, can be seen when Catherine likens the soul to a fortified city protected by three main gates: memory, understanding, and will. Free choice, she says, stands guard at the gate of the will, and "if it so chooses, always holds firm and guards the others." Then, all the gates of the city remain secure and "one sweet sound comes forth from the city of the soul." (D. 144:299; 147:310)

Catherine further integrates her symbols when she equates the stairway of Christ's body with the three human powers, "I have also shown you the three ordinary stairs," she says, "that is, the soul's three powers." (D. 55:109) In each of the stages, or at each of the stairs, the memory, understanding, and will evolve to an increasingly profound level of harmony.[27] The essence of Catherine's entire spiritual way is contained in this harmonizing of her three human powers to reflect the unity of the Trinity; she emphasizes that these powers enable each individual to be the architect of his/her own soul.[28] Their transformation provides the underlying dynamic of rising by means of the stairs:

> I have explained the image of the three stairs for you in general in terms of the soul's three powers. These are three stairs, none of which can be climbed without the others if one wishes to go the way of the teaching, the bridge, of my Truth. Nor can the soul persevere without uniting these three powers as one. (D. 52:105)

Like the divine Trinity which they mirror, the powers are inseparable, though distinct; therefore, they must develop in unison. Similarly, in the symbolism, one stair cannot be climbed without climbing the others. By mounting the stairs again and again, not repetitively as in a cycle, but with the vibrant propelling motion of the spiral, Catherine's internal being will become unified. Only in this way, will she achieve the mirror image of the oneness of Godhead.

In the first step to mirror the Trinity the memory predominates as, similar to the creative power of the Father, it is the initiator. Affection fills Catherine's memory with thoughts of God's blessings and goodness and kindles desire so that she becomes "caring instead of indifferent" and "grateful instead of thankless." Yet, memory alone cannot create desire without the cooperation of the understanding and the will. Thus, understanding, contemplating these remembrances of God's love, is also flooded with desire. The will then chooses to join memory and understanding in knowing and loving the object of their desire. The three, having fostered change in each other, thus cooperate in their choice to love God above every passing thing. (D. 50: 103; 54: 108) "Open up our memory for us," she begs, "so that we may receive, hold fast, and understand God's great goodness! For as we understand, so we love. . . ."[29]

"When these three powers of your soul are gathered together," God tells Catherine, "I am in their midst by grace." (D. 54: 108) The effects of this divine interior indwelling resemble those already mentioned: like the roots of the tree, Catherine is ready to rise above herself. She is "in the company of the multitude of solid virtues." She thirsts with the great desire of one who has climbed the first step of affection. Exercising her free choice, she wills to go forward.

At the second step, the redemptive wisdom of the Son predominates to accomplish the enlightenment of Catherine's understanding. "Once we see ourselves so boundlessly loved, . . . the fire floods us with light," she says, "leaving no room for darkness" and "enlightened by that venerable fire, our understanding expands and opens wide."[30] No human effort can achieve this end, just as no human effort could have achieved salvation without the mediation of the divine Redeemer. Hence, it is the wisdom of the open wounded heart of the Son that enlightens Catherine's understanding to know that she, too, must become redeemer. She must become responsible, not only for her own sanctification, but also for the salvation of her neighbor. "They know my truth," God says, "when their understanding — which is the soul's eye — is enlightened in me." (D. 45:92)

In a letter to Fra Bartolomeo, Catherine reflects the dynamic of this understanding in a meditation on the words, "God is Love." They teach her, she says, to look with the eyes of love into Christ's loving heart. "Let your memory open up at once to receive what your understanding has seen in his divine love, she instructs him, "and let your will rise up in blazing desire to receive and gaze upon the burning heart of the giver."[31] Her desire is to see Bartolomeo set afire, "swallowed up and consumed" in the blazing charity of the heart of Christ until he will "lose all self-consciousness" so that he will be "freed from all suffering and grief," and "clothed in the fiery blood" of God's Son.

At the heart of Christ Catherine's three powers come together in "the enlightenment of the mind." When the mind sees itself "reflected in the warm hearted love" of Christ crucified "as in a mirror," the "memory is filled with light from understanding and the overflowing love of the will."[32] (D. 54:108) The discernment which accompanies enlightenment helps Catherine to place consolation and trial in proper balance and to be concerned more with God than with her own comfort. When she understands God's immense love for her, she sees that it is not any effort of her own that makes her worthy but only God. Then, "with spiritual gladness and joy," she can accept "whatever God sends in reverent love." (D. 71:133-134)

The wisdom to discern spirits follows the enlightenment of the mind. Catherine learns to distinguish between a visitation from the devil and one from God.[33] The devil comes, she says, with gladness, but soon the gladness gives way to weariness, confusion, and darkness as the understanding is clouded over by the presence of evil. (D. 71:134) A visitation from God begins in fear but the middle and the end hold gladness and hunger for virtue. Even the initial fear holds "gladness and security" for it comes from the awe of the creature for the Creator. This awe introduces "a gentle prudence that does not doubt even while it doubts." (D. 71:134)

Finally, Catherine learns that even as she is loved, so God loves every other human being. Loving her neighbor, then, is the only return that Catherine can make to her Creator; her love for God will be measured by the love with which she loves her neighbor. Catherine is fired with desire to enter into the redemptive work of the Son. The human, however, must freely choose to actualize her call to redemptive love; therefore, the will leads her to complete her union with God. At Christ's mouth, when Catherine enters into Godhead as into "a peaceful sea," her union is so intense that she "knows no movement" but in God. (D. 78:145-147) In this unrestricted integration of her memory, understanding, and will, "the memory finds itself filled with nothing but God. The understanding is lifted up as it gazes into Truth. The will, which always follows the understanding, loves and unites itself with what the eye of understanding sees." (D. 79:148) Catherine says that "like the burning coal that no one can put out once it is completely consumed in the furnace," she has "been turned into fire." (D. 78:147) "This fire is the love that is the Holy Spirit," Catherine declares. [34]

She speaks of her desire to be filled with the object of her longing and the necessity to leave behind "the body's heaviness" which imprisons her spirit. Her love has become so overwhelming that it demands total identification:

> When we look into ourselves and see there such a marvelous strength as is this fire, the Holy Spirit, we become so

drunk with love for our Creator that we completely lose ourselves. We live as if we were dead, feeling within ourselves no creaturely love or pleasure, since our memory is already filled with love for our Creator. Our understanding . . . sees and understands only our own nothingness and God's goodness to us. . . . Now our love for God has become perfect . . . now there is no holding back the swift course of desire. . . . And we are so yoked with Christ that we love ourselves for God, and God for God, and our neighbors for God. [35]

Having entered the mouth of union, Catherine says that she chews with two rows of teeth, hatred of sin and love of virtue; she tastes and savors the fruit of her labor until the food reaches to the stomach, prepared by desire and hunger for souls to receive it. The richness of this food makes her grow so fat that her body bursts, she splits apart, and finally she dies to herself. (D. 76:140) Thus, she reaches a culminating point of the spiritual life described in the *Dialogue* as the death of the will:

Then the soul grows so fat on true and solid virtues and so big because of the abundance of this food that the garment of selfish sensuality (that is, the body which covers the soul) splits apart so far as its sensual appetite is concerned. Now anyone who splits apart dies. So the sensual will is dead. Because the soul's well-ordered will is alive in me, clothed in my eternal will, her sensual will is dead. (D. 76:141)

Catherine calls this phenomenon lightness of spirit. "Though she is mortal she tastes the reward of the immortals, and weighed down still with the body she receives the lightness of the spirit." (D. 79:147-148) She carefully distinguishes between physical death and spiritual death when she states, "the soul does not really leave the body (this happens only in death)." She attributes this union to the harmony in which "her powers and emotions are united" with God in love. God says, "The body was a barrier to their knowing the truth perfectly. They could not see me face to face without leaving the body behind." (D. 45:91-92) Catherine describes her experience in precise language:

> [T]he soul attains such union that she hardly knows whether she is in the body or out. She tastes the pledge of eternal life through her union with me because her will is dead. It is by that death that she realizes her union with me, and in no other way could she perfectly accomplish that. (D. 85:158)

The convergence of Catherine's human will with God's will accomplishes such a harmony during lightness of spirit that, though she remains alert, her senses no longer function normally:

> When these powers are gathered and united all together and immersed and set afire in me, the body loses its feeling. For the eye sees without seeing; the ear hears without hearing; the tongue speaks without speaking . . . the hand touches without touching; the feet walk without walking. All the members are bound and busied with the bond and feeling of love. (D. 79:148)

At the conclusion of this experience, Catherine awakens with a longing for physical death so that this wondrous state of union can be permanent. However, she is content to live and work for the glory of God in this world because her will is so attuned to the divine will. God always remains within her, but not with the continuing intensity of lightness of spirit because the body is "not capable of bearing such a union constantly." (D. 84:154-155) The energy released by this "setting afire" of her whole being will affect Catherine for the remainder of her life, impelling her to love her neighbor as she loves the image of the triune Godhead within herself.

Mirroring the oneness of the Trinitarian Godhead, gathered together in unity, and drawn by love, everything Catherine does is in total harmony with her Creator. (D. 26:65) Knowing God's love for all creatures, how they, too, reflect God's likeness, she so "falls in love" with the beauty of God's people that she feels "unbearable sorrow" when she sees them stray from God's goodness, a suffering so great that it makes "every other suffering diminish." (D. 145:306) Suffering with the redemptive Christ for the benefit of her neighbor is the key to her union with God.

Catherine's expression of this reality in the *Dialogue* is a convincing example of her power of symbolic integration. She condenses into one message her spirituality of Trinitarian harmony, Christ's two great commandments — to love God and her neighbor as she loves herself — and Matthew 18:20: "If two or three or more are gathered in my name, I shall be in their midst." These two commandments, she states, "cannot be gathered together in my name without three — that is the gathering together of the three powers of the soul: memory, understanding, and will." (D. 54:108) One must, she teaches, achieve the unity of the three in the one of the Trinity in order to accomplish the dual command to love both God and neighbor:

> I have told you . . . "Whenever two or three or more are gathered in my name" — how this is the gathering of these three stairs, the soul's three powers. When these three powers are in harmony they have with them the two chief commandments of the Law, love of me and love of your neighbor, that is, to love me above all things and your neighbor as your very self. (D. 55:109)

Moreover, Catherine can only express her love for God through her neighbor. She is told, "I ask you to love me with the same love with which I love you." However, this is impossible because, "Whatever love you have for me you owe me, so you love me not gratuitously but out of duty." (D. 64:121) Only by gratuitous love extended to her neighbors, can Catherine repay the unmerited love that God showers on her. "You know," she wrote, "we cannot show this love without some medium, and this medium is our neighbor."[36]

> This is why I have put you among your neighbors: so that you can do for them what you cannot do for me — that is, love them without any concern for thanks and without looking for any profit for yourself. And whatever you do for them I will consider done for me. (D. 64:121)

Constant work for the salvation of souls and the honor and glory of God become Catherine's only joy as she attempts to live out the unity of her will with that of her Creator.

ENDNOTES

1. *Letters*, 62, pp. 198-199.
2. *I, Catherine*, Letter 31, p. 145.
3. Ibid., p. 146.
4. *Letters*, 62, p. 198.
5. Ibid.
6. In her letter Catherine equates affection with desire, "just as the feet carry the body, desire carries the soul." Ibid.
7. Ibid.
8. *I, Catherine*, Letter 31, p. 145.
9. *Letters*, 62, pp. 198-199.
10. Ibid., 3, p. 44.
11. Bennett, "Conscious Labor and Intentional Suffering."
12. *Letters*, 62, p. 199.
13. Ibid.
14. Ibid., 3, p. 44.
15. During this period of open conflict — an example of the way in which Catherine had become known outside Siena — she received a letter from a Florentine, a total stranger, criticizing her eating habits. Catherine's response conveyed her own interpretation of her problem: "You have sent me word to pray to God particularly that I might eat. I tell you, my father, and I say it in the sight of God, that in all ways within my power I have always forced myself once or twice a day to take food. And I have prayed constantly, and do pray God and shall pray Him, that in this matter of eating He will give me the grace to live like other creatures, if it is His will — for it is mine. . . . I for myself do not know what other remedy to adopt. . . . I beg you that if you see any remedy you will write me of it." Scudder, p. 78.

16. Many women who had ruined their health and remained sick for the remainder of their lives because of fasting and flagellation, learned to cease such practices; in their mature years these saints always discouraged others from such self-mortification. Petroff, pp. 42-43. See, for example, this letter to her close friend Alessa; Catherine gave specific directions: "I beg and command you not to fast, except when you can, on the days commanded by the Holy Church. And when you do not feel strong enough to fast then, do not observe them. At other times, do not fast, except when you feel able, on Saturday. When this heat is over, fast on the days of Holy Mary, if you can, and no more. And drink something beside water every day. Labor hard to increase your holy desire, and let these other things alone for the future." Scudder, p. 71.

17. God reminded Catherine in the *Dialogue* of a day she came to the church and was refused communion by the celebrant: "The tears and longing grew in her; and in him, when he came to the offering of the chalice, the pricking of conscience grew, urged on by that servant, the Holy Spirit, who was providing for that soul. . . . the priest said to the server, 'Ask her if she wants to receive communion, for I will willingly give it to her.' And if she had the tiniest bit of faith and love before, it now grew to overflowing fullness with such great longing that it seemed as if the life wanted to leave her body." D. 142:294. See also D. 111:210-211; 142:294-295.

18. As "the visionaries are moving away from a personal, problem-oriented stage," they "find themselves more in demand by others." They begin to acquire "a reputation for having a special relationship with the divine," reinforcing their "new and powerful identity." They have attained the "status of a prophetess, a seer" though in their own eyes they are less significant than before. Petroff, pp. 53, 55, 56.

19. *I, Catherine*, Letter 5, pp. 61-64; *Letters*, 23, p. 91.

20. *Letters*, 20, p. 81.

21. Ibid.

22. Ibid., 22, p. 86.

23. The indecisiveness of Tommaso dalla Fonte in all of these situations brought unnecessary suffering to Catherine — though their friendship endured to her death. The responsibility placed on this young cleric must have weighed heavily as Catherine became a public figure about whom everyone had an opinion. Though unsure how to guide her, he was certainly aware of her extraordinary sanctity and kept careful notes of all her experiences. It appears that his health failed before the resolution of Catherine's status and the appointment of Raymond as official confessor. When he was recuperating just outside of Siena, Catherine wrote an encouraging letter dated May, 1374, which referred to Tommaso's state of indecision: "It seems you are proposing to go somewhere else. It did not seem to me that you ought to do this now; however, be it done according to God's will and yours. May God grant you to choose what is best in this. . . ." *I, Catherine*, Letter 1, p. 53.

24. Looking to the theology of her own time, Catherine turned to Saint Augustine whose well known thesis, *De Trinitate*, had first suggested the human mind with its tripartite powers of memory, understanding, and will as the most perfect created image of the Trinity. *The Trinity*, McKenna, ed., vii, xi.

25. Discussing self-evolution, Nicoll states, "it is only the inner, unorganized side of a man which can evolve as does a seed by its own growth, from itself . . . [it must] be capable of penetrating more deeply and awakening the man himself — the inner unorganized man. A man evolves internally through his deeper reflection, not through his outer life-controlled self. He evolves through the spirit of his individual understanding and by inner consent to what he sees as truth." p. 4.

26. *I, Catherine*, Letter 40, p. 180.
27. Nicoll's interpretation of psychological inner language, which evolves as a seed from within a person, contains three stages as well: the first stage of growth to wisdom contains allusions similar to the gathering of the three powers. "He must hear it; but this does not mean merely to hear it literally, but to begin to understand it, to hear it with his mind, to ponder it, to think of its meaning, to take it into his inner consciousness and to see himself in terms of what it teaches." p. 69.
28. *Letters*, 55, p. 172.
29. Ibid., 3, p. 44.
30. Ibid., 51, p. 155.
31. Ibid., 27, p. 98.
32. Parallel to Catherine's enlightenment of the mind is Nicoll's slow preparation of the mind for change "because this higher level is different from a lower level and so the thoughts belonging to a lower level are not of the same order as those of a higher level. Something new must be formed in his mind to receive 'light' — so he must gradually come to think in a new way.' " p. 69.
33. Catherine's description of the discernment of spirits is similar to Ignatius of Loyola's attention to the beginning, middle, and end of a spiritual experience, as well as to the emotional content of a good and an evil visitation. See *The Spiritual Exercises of St. Ignatius of Loyola*, tr. by Louis J. Puhl, S.J., Loyola University Press, 1951, pp. 147-150.
34. *Letters*, 84, p. 255.
35. Ibid.
36. Ibid., 40, p. 131.

7

EVERY GOOD WORK
IS DONE THROUGH YOUR NEIGHBOR

Each image portraying Catherine's spiritual journey describes an initial inward movement that eventually thrusts outward. The roots and marrow of her tree must grow strong before blossoms and fruit appear. The lights of discernment first lead her to recognize the proper relational attitude between herself and God, then self, God, and neighbor. The isolated reasoning powers gradually fuse in a concerted energy that leads first to love, then to wisdom, and finally to total incorporation into Godhead. Then, Catherine feels such "a stinging hunger" for the salvation of her neighbor that she is fired by a compassion which cries for release lest it burst the bounds of the human spirit. This burning compassion leads Catherine to the choice incumbent upon every true mystic, to bring her deep interior experience to bear upon the world in which she lives.[1] Solitude and separation no longer suffice. Prayer and service, contemplation and action become equal manifestations of worship. Loving and serving the neighbor is loving and serving God.

Catherine's symbolic expression of this change of the focus of her love follows the inward-outward pattern of her previous symbols. The tree of virtue now becomes the tree of the cross, and the lights of discernment realized in the harmony of the three rational powers conclude in a series of bridal images. Giving birth to virtue, dressing in bridal clothing, participating in the banquet of the cross, and eating the food of souls express Catherine's concept of being a spouse to the Godhead. These images clarify and integrate the activity she has attributed to the stages of her spiritual journey.

The Wedding Garment of Charity

On reaching full bloom, the symbolic tree of virtue produced flowers of virtues and fruits of action. Now, having reached spiritual maturity, Catherine, too, is ready to flower and bear fruit. However, just as there is a difference between the nature of a flower and the nature of a fruit, so, too, she makes a distinction between one who "conceives virtue for her neighbor" and one who "gives birth." "Conceive" implies an intention; like betrothal, this is a promise of what is to come. Only when she gives birth is she a true spouse; only then may she don the wedding garment and come to the banquet of the cross:

> I am the spouse of the soul, and unless she gives birth to the
> virtue she has conceived by showing it in her charity to her
> neighbors in their general and individual needs in the ways I
> have described, then I insist that she has never in truth
> even conceived virtue within her. (D. 11:45)

Until charity toward her neighbor becomes a reality, there is only promise and anticipation. Indeed, in the *Dialogue* God declares, "If a woman has conceived a child but never brings it to birth for people to see, her husband will consider himself childless." (D. 11:45) "What I want," God says, "is many works of patient and courageous endurance . . . interior virtues that are all active in bearing the fruit of grace." (D. 11:42) Giving birth as a true spouse also follows a three staged development:

> At the first step, they put off love of vice from the feet of
> their affection. At the second they taste the secret and the

love of his heart and there conceive love in virtue. At the
third step of spiritual peace and calm they prove their
virtue, and rising from imperfect love they come to great
perfection. (D. 78:145)

Virtue must first benefit Catherine herself; she must conceive the virtue that will produce the life of grace in her. Different
responsibilities will then follow. In giving birth, she will reach out
to "the whole world's need for salvation" with a general love for all
people; she will give special attention to the "specific needs of her
neighbors"; and she will come to the aid of "those nearest her."
All this will be done according to the graces God has "given her for
ministry," a ministry that includes both word and example. She
will give "sincere and impartial counsel," and edify her neighbor
"by her good, holy, honorable life." (D. 7:37)

In carrying out this mandate, however, Catherine's difficulties with the Sienese Friars and the Sisters of Penance
presented a serious problem. Their objections to her public
activities placed serious strains on her validity; their attempts to
prevent her from attending meetings, and to deprive her of holy
communion, confession, and a confessor — tantamount to dis-
missal from the group — threatened to deprive her of a position
within the Church. (L. 365) No one would have been more aware
than Catherine that a loss of her official third order standing within
the Dominican community would seriously jeopardize the apostolate to which she was divinely called, a call which could be
actualized neither as a cloistered religious nor as a private lay
woman.

In a General Chapter of the Dominican Order convened in
Florence in May of 1374, the Master General of the Order, Elias
of Toulouse resolved Catherine's difficult situation by appointing
Raymond of Capua as her official confessor. [2] It is not unlikely that
Catherine's influential friends brought her plight to the attention
of highly placed Dominicans or even to Raymond's personal

attention since her reputation was already well established, even at the papal court.[3] Raymond had held important positions in the Order and had a reputation in matters of extraordinary sanctity as a learned theologian and man of experience. Therefore, his official appointment, together with his credentials as a highly reputable scholar, theologian, and spiritual director, brought a measure of order to Catherine's external existence and permitted her to carry out the ministry to which she was called.[4]

Criticism and conflict were never far from Catherine; they continually seared her soul. Opportunity to practice patience, "lest it grow rusty," never diminished. (D. 145:305) A passage in the *Dialogue* regarding jealousy among the "foolish, proud, and learned" has an autobiographical tone. While affirming that the spiritual counsel of a humble person with a holy and upright conscience surpasses that of a well read but proud scholar, she admonishes learned people who "wonder and fall to whining when they see so many uncultured and unschooled in biblical knowledge yet as enlightened in knowledge of the truth as if they had studied for a long time." (D. 85:157)

The pain that Catherine endured during this period of conflict in Siena always remained with her. A reference in her correspondence to the subject of her travel reveals her attitude:

> always fulfilling God's sweet will in myself — in going and staying — not that of men . . . I neither stay, nor go on wearisome journeys . . . out of pleasure, but only when compelled by God, for his honor and the salvation of souls. Nor can I do otherwise, even if such hearts choose to draw evil out of good.[5]

She recalled her own experience when she wrote to encourage a young Mantellate of Orvieto who was troubled by a confessor who prevented her from doing what she felt called to do by God. She confessed, "I know of nothing so wearisome as distress of this kind," because while one "cannot resist God," one would like to obey his servants, "trusting their light and knowledge more than its own; but it does not seem able to." She then reveals her own determination never to let "resolutions, or silence, or anything else, stand in the way" because "our one principle and foundation is love of God and love of neighbor."[6]

The *Dialogue* confirms an interior change in Catherine. Growing strong, she does not seek her own comfort, "for the fear she had of not showing herself lest she lose her own consolation is gone . . . she has come to perfect, free love, she lets go of herself and comes out." (D. 74:136-137) This perfect love is the love of the Holy Spirit, which makes her will "strong to endure suffering and to leave her house . . . to give birth to the virtues for her neighbors." This love is also gratuitous and compassionate so that Catherine is able to give birth to virtue in the ways that her neighbors need them. Catherine responds to the command of God expressed in the *Dialogue*:

> I have set you as workers in your own and your neighbors'
> souls and in the mystic body of Holy Church. In yourselves
> you must work at virtue; in your neighbors and in the
> Church you must work by example and teaching. And you
> must offer me constant prayer for the Church and for every
> creature, giving birth to virtue through your neighbors. For
> I have already told you that every virtue and every sin is
> realized and intensified through your neighbors. Therefore,
> I want you to serve your neighbors and in this way share the
> fruits of your own vineyard. (D. 86:159)

Impelled by this motivating principle, Catherine refuses to be held back by "disgrace, insults, mockery, abuse, and reproach." She continually instructs her disciples in love for one another, and in "a great and true compassion" which "gives birth to the other by desire" with sighs, tears and unceasing prayer.[7] And she instructs them how to "bear fruit," by following the example of Christ who first practiced virtue and then preached

it.[8] "Virtue once conceived, must come to birth" she says; and so
it does with all the pain that birth implies, for God promised to
purify her so that she would produce better and sweeter fruit.

At a more deeply symbolic level, Catherine adds to her
interpretation of spousal relationship to God through her neighbor. A passage in the *Dialogue* makes it clear that the love which
leads to union develops gradually and progressively. Relating her
symbolism of the stairs to clothing, Catherine states:

> At the first stair, lifting the feet of her affections from the
> earth, she stripped herself of sin. At the second she dres-
> sed herself in love for virtue. (D. 26:65)

In a similar manner, Catherine expresses another activity of the
first two stages — when love overpowers fear — in an account of
the experience of a soul: "at first fear enters in and strips it of
vice, then Love fills it and clothes it with virtue."[9] She also makes
an explicit distinction between God's gift — creation in God's
image — and dressing in the garment of charity:

> But beyond the beauty I have given the soul by creating her
> in my image and likeness, look at those who are clothed in
> the wedding garment of charity, adorned with many true
> virtues. (D. 1:26)

References to the clothing of charity in Catherine's letters
delineate her meaning further. According to her, whoever follows
the way of Christ crucified is clothed in the gleaming garment of
charity, the ground of all the virtues.[10] With this clothing, the soul
becomes "so strong that no dart can strike home but rebounds at
whoever threw it."[11] She tells Raymond that the wedding garment is a suit of armor that deflects the blows of the enemy
[Satan], blows which become "precious stones and pearls set into
this garment of blazing charity."[12] She further advises that he
wrap himself "so tightly in this garment as to make it a second

skin that can never be stripped from you until you are stripped of life itself."[13]

In the *Dialogue*, when God says of those clothed in the garment of charity, "They are united with me through love," Catherine confirms that donning this garment is a step toward union. The words that follow, "If you should ask me who they are, I would answer . . . that they are another me," indicate the quality of the union which this charity brings about. Then, Catherine's interpretation penetrates to the deepest expression of union, "They have lost and drowned their own will and have clothed themselves and united themselves and conformed themselves with mine." (D. 1:26) Thus, the interior transformation in Catherine's life that is so critical to the life of union — willing what God wills for her — is effectively mirrored in the image of clothing. The charity that weaves a wedding garment requires the merger of Catherine's will with God's will.

She has already described the effects of this merger as an experience of "lightness of spirit" in which she attains such a union that she hardly knows whether or not she is in her body. In this merger, "the perfection of this unitive state," Catherine says she is "carried off by the fire of charity" which brings with it "supernatural insight"[14] and is "clothed in perfect light . . . in a new nature, the gentle Christ Jesus." (D. 85:157-158; 100:189) She compares this experience in which one "sees, knows, and is clothed with the Truth"[15] to that of the Apostles who, on Pentecost, were "clothed with the fire of his charity" so that "their one desire was to offer to all men the truth by which they themselves had been enlightened."[16]

To this point, her ardent desire for union, like the desire to conceive virtue, imbues the clothing image with a sense of betrothal or promise. Now, with the addition of the Pentecostal fire of the Spirit, desire becomes a thirst for action, a willingness and receptivity to become an instrument for giving birth or proving virtue through her neighbor. Since the requisite virtue for the active life is patience, it is the exercise of this virtue — the very heart of charity — that determines "whether the mantle of this charity is a wedding garment or not." Only when these two virtues are "woven together in trial and conflict," is Catherine ready for the wedding feast. (D. 95:178) "By enduring with true patience until death . . . and accepting patiently any injury done to ourselves," Catherine declares, one is prepared "to climb up to the table of the cross, and there partake of the food of souls for the honor of God."[17]

The need to wear a wedding garment to approach this table implies a bridal feast, and making the table synonymous with the cross reveals that to participate in the feast requires an acceptance of the suffering of Christ's passion. To be spouse, then, is to be a victim for humanity as Christ was and like him "to eat the food of God's honor and the salvation of souls at the table of the cross." In addition, Catherine says, this food cannot be eaten "anywhere but on the cross" where "the Son of God himself simultaneously endured physical torment and the agony of desire."[18] Christ's desire, she says, exacted the more costly sacrifice; hence, Catherine refers to the cross as a table of desire where "seated with the Bridegroom at the table of crucified desire," she can delight "in seeking God's honor and the salvation of souls."[19]

These images suggest a connection between the wedding banquet and the Eucharistic altar of sacrifice where the food is the body of Christ. Catherine urges frequent communion, "so that, made strong in this life of pilgrimage, you may run manfully to the table of the cross by way of the doctrine of the humble Lamb, and there partake of the sweet angelic food."[20] Similarly, there is an implied correlation between the three-tiered action of the stairs and the Eucharistic liturgy in which one steps up to the altar of sacrifice repenting for sin, reaches the heart in the breaking of the bread, and completes the sacrifice by feeding on the Body and Blood of Christ.

In the dynamic of the stairs, Catherine "takes her place" at the table of the cross when she turns from vice to the love and practice of virtue. (D. 95:177) She begins to "prepare" her table when, opening her heart to the transforming power of Christ's love, she chooses to walk in the footsteps of Christ crucified and to participate in the mystery of redemption. (D. 95:177) Then, filled with overpowering love, she rushes to the banquet table to "feed" at the table of the most holy cross, that is, to pattern herself "after the humble, patient, spotless Lamb, my only-begotten Son." (D. 100:189; 89:163)

The wedding feast celebrates Catherine's participation in the ongoing drama of redemption. Her hunger for "souls," the food served at the table of the cross, is an expression of Christ's own crucifying desire to save humankind. Like Christ, Catherine will be both victim and advocate; she is at once the food that is assimilated, and she also eats the food of souls to save them. Through the medium of her neighbor, Catherine identifies the ministry that will occupy the remainder of her life. Entrance into the peaceful sea of Christ's mouth taught her that "the tongue of holy and constant prayer" has an interior and exterior language. In interior contemplative prayer, she will raise "tender loving desires for the salvation of souls," and in exterior activity, she will proclaim Christ's teachings, "admonishing, advising, and testifying," adapting her "enthusiastic testimony to the situation of each person she confronts." (D. 76:140)

Tasting God's "loving charity" arouses such a thirst to accomplish God's will in herself and in all others that Catherine thirsts for the good of her neighbor, hungering to reach out with the message of love to God's people and for God's Church. (D. 76:141) This hunger for God's honor and the salvation of souls, makes "the soul run to the table of crucified desire" to eat "such quantities of this sweet wholesome food that it bursts . . . leaving the will quite dead." The discerning insight by which Catherine recognizes the inseparable unity in loving God and her neighbor brings her to a lightness of spirit, the death to self in which her will is fused into Godhead as the coal becomes one with the fire in the furnace. Ultimately, she joins God at the table of the cross. Feasting there, suffering with the redemptive Christ, is the key to her continuous union with God:

> I tell you, these beloved children of mine who have attained the highest perfection through perseverance and watching and constant humble prayer show me that they love me in truth . . . by following this holy teaching of my Truth in their suffering and in the burdens they bear for their neighbor's salvation. They have found no other way than this to show their love for me. Indeed, any other way there may be to show their love is based on this principal way, for every good work is done through your neighbors. (D. 145:304)

Running Along the Bridge

When Catherine returned from the meeting of the Dominican General Chapter in Florence, Siena was once again ravaged by a wave of the Black Death. She and her followers spent the summer tending to the sick and dying. In the fall of 1374, Catherine accepted a long standing invitation to go to Pisa.[21] Enjoying new freedom in her outer life, she prayed for guidance and asked Raymond's permission to make the journey. The request was granted, and she set off in the company of Raymond, Tommaso, and several of the Sienese Mantellate. (L. 232, 234) This was the first of many journeys Catherine would make "always fulfilling God's sweet will." The joy that she feels in assuming her active ministry is expressed in her symbolism of "running." She runs along the bridge, entered by the three stairs, toward final and permanent union.

Catherine speaks of the bridge as the fourth stage of the spiritual life in which "she both tastes and gives birth to charity in the person of her neighbor." The third and fourth stages, she

says, "are linked together." One is never found without the other "any more than charity for me can exist without charity for one's neighbor or the latter without charity for me. The one cannot be separated from the other." (D. 74:137)

The fourth stage is a permanent one. Climbing and reclimbing the stairs provide continuous opportunity to grow more perfect. However, traveling along the bridge means living a life of continuous union. Catherine "runs briskly along the way of the teaching of Christ crucified" in great patience, without slowing her pace or stopping because of persecution or pleasure. This patience, God says, "is a sure sign that the soul loves me perfectly and without self-interest, for if she loved me and her neighbors for her own profit she would be impatient and slacken her pace." (D. 76:141)

The bridge stretches between heaven and earth — reminiscent of the tree of virtue — to join "the earth of your humanity with the greatness of the Godhead." This path to salvation is available to every person desirous of eternal life and, like the image of the stairs, has the body of Christ crucified as its central focus. But, in keeping with Catherine's teaching that one divine person cannot be present without the other, the bridge also assumes Trinitarian aspects. (D. 22:59)

Catherine weaves together all the isolated elements of Christ's teachings, his human and divine nature, his life, passion, death, and resurrection into this one embracing symbol. She explains that the path from heaven to earth remained broken and impassable after Adam's sin until Christ's atoning sacrifice, his crucifixion and resurrection, repaired and reopened it. Then, Christ's body became a bridge raised between heaven and earth as a redemptive gift to humankind. The bridge — Christ's teaching as well as his body — is "the way, the truth, and the life" promised in scripture. [22]

Stones, symbols of the virtues Christ modelled in life, line the bridge and form walls for safety, all held in place by the mortar of Christ's blood. The mercy of the Spirit covers over the bridge with its protective love; at hostels along the way, the food of the body and blood of Christ provides nourishment. The bridge terminates in the gate to heaven, also Christ, in fulfillment of his word that no one can go to the Father except through him. [23] Passing through the gate, one enters into the Father who says in the *Dialogue*, "And I am one with the gate and the way that is my Son. . . ." (D. 27:66-67) Thus, the symbolism of the bridge verifies the significance of the Trinity in Catherine's thought and figures the triune nature of the salvation story: the Son teaches, gives living example, redeems, feeds, and is the path itself; the Spirit loves, protects, and oversees; and the Father, one with the Son and Spirit, is both the path, the gate, and the goal of the journey.

Running along the bridge, Catherine enters into her public life in response to the divine mandate to love her neighbor gratuitously as the medium of her love for God. In so doing she exercises the virtues which crowned the tip of her tree of virtue: patience, courage, and perseverance. These are the virtues which enable Catherine to bear fruit: preaching Christ's truth and admonishing and advising her neighbor as testimony of God's loving mercy for them and for the world. In a letter to Cardinal Corsini at Avignon, Catherine's view of good preaching comes through clearly. She states, "When you speak and proclaim the truth, whether in giving counsel or in any other role, do it fearlessly," adding, "I want you to be a lion roaring loudly in Holy Church, your virtue and your voice so strong that you help bring back life to the children lying dead within her."[24]

Following in Christ's footsteps, Catherine does as she advises a Bishop; she loses her fear to correct others and administers spiritual favors to her neighbors as they have been given to her, freely. [25] From gentle Jesus, her teacher and guide, she learns never to look for anything but the Father's honor and the salvation of her neighbor. [26] She takes courage from the dramatic change which took place in the apostles after the coming of the Holy Spirit. Like them, she, too, is made strong in mind by the fire of the Spirit so that she can testify to Christ's truth and offer reproof to sinners. (D. 29:69) Like them, she becomes a human agent of the Spirit who uses "mortal creatures" subject to every weakness so that people can change their ways before it is too late. (D. 36:78)

In Mary Magdalene, Catherine finds a model who has no thought of herself, of prestige, grandeur, pleasure or delight. Magdalene, she says, embraces the path of lowliness, leaves aside self-consciousness, and thinks only of how she can follow Jesus. [27] Magdalene shows great courage at the foot of the cross and models perseverance in seeking Jesus in the tomb even when she has no idea where he has been buried. On fire with love for her Master, she puts this love into action by preaching to her neighbor after Christ's resurrection. [28] So, too, does Catherine.

As testimony to the success of her ministry, Raymond recorded that "endless streams of men and women" flocked to see or hear her "as though summoned by an invisible trumpet." By papal brief he and two companions who traveled with her received "faculties equivalent to a bishop's" to absolve everyone who wished to confess their sins after hearing her preach. (L. 217) There is also Catherine's own reference to the jealousy that greeted the successful teaching of a humble unschooled person. (D. 85:157) As tangible evidence of Catherine's public ministry, not only do we have access to many of her letters, but the *Dialogue* explicitly recounts her request for guidance when "people will come to me . . . asking for counsel in their desire to serve you and wanting me to instruct them." (D. 97:182) In response, three principles of direction appear in the section of the *Dialogue* entitled "Truth."

The first instruction cautioned Catherine always to qualify her judgment of any person despite the appearance of sin and to make corrections in a general way without confronting specific failings. Rather, she should plant virtue in a loving, kind way and discourage vice by silence or by a holy argument, always accusing herself of the same vice in true humility. (D. 102:193-194) The second principle directed Catherine never to judge her neighbor since judgment was the prerogative of God alone. Neither was she to presume the presence or the absence of grace in a person from the presence of desolation rather than consolation since God reminded her that each of these gifts could be present in a person who was wholly conformed to the divine will. The discernment of God's will was more important than judging other people's intentions. (D. 103:194-195) The third principle addresses the unique differences in individuals. Catherine was cautioned not to direct all persons to walk by the same path that she did. What was important was that each one be encouraged to immerse his/her own will into the divine will. (D. 104:196-197)

Whether communicating with ordinary persons desirous of changing their personal lifestyle, with heads of state, or with Church leaders, Catherine adhered to these principles of direction in a remarkable way. Her non-judgmental stance enabled her to describe a virtuous option without accusation of vice since her basic assumption was of good intention in each individual. Most remarkable was her sensitivity to the spiritual capability of her subjects to respond to her prodding. Though she called all to the maximum effort of which they were capable, she never placed on anyone the expectation that she demanded of herself.

Eating souls and giving birth to them is the public ministry that unites Catherine to the sacrifice of the cross. This exterior activity is "continuous" prayer, "that abiding holy desire which prays to God in everything we creatures do."[29] When she refers to continuous prayer in the *Dialogue* she states, "there are times when prayer means service . . . as charity asks . . . according to the need . . . and the situation in which I have placed her." In this instance, she insists, "Whatever you do in word or in deed for the good of your neighbor is real prayer," and "every time and place is a time and place of prayer." (D. 66:126-127;74:137)

Just as assiduously, she eats souls and gives birth by her prayer for them. Catherine contends that the highest level of interior prayer, one that "lifts itself above the crude level of feeling and with the mind of an angel is made one with God," is "a mother, conceiving her children, the virtues," and "giving birth to them in love for others."[30] Hence, she writes Raymond, "This soul of yours has become my food, not a moment passes that I am not eating this food at the table of the gentle Lamb. . . ."[31] Advising a Mantellate to seek the seclusion of her cell, she tells her, "there apply yourself in love and holy desire to eating souls and giving them birth in the sight of God."[32] She writes to a Carthusian monk, "I am continually giving you birth by prayer and desire in God's presence just as truly as a mother gives birth to her child."[33] She even instructs the mother of her disciple, Stephano Maconi, "You, his mother, gave birth to him once; now I want to give birth to him and to you and to your family . . . by my constant prayers and desire for your salvation."[34]

Where now, is the child of the vision? Fear, self-interest, and self-will have been swallowed up by love and desire, by the wisdom of suffering, and by the triumph of charity and patience. Their offspring, courage and perseverance, lead Catherine to run along the bridge to salvation, preaching, teaching, counseling, and admonishing without fear in a public ministry of continuous prayer coupled with interior prayer; like love of God and love of neighbor the two forms of prayer are inseparable. In each she eats and gives birth to souls.

Thus Catherine, "inebriated and set on fire and sated with holy longing" is, like the coal in the furnace, totally consumed in fire. (D. 66:123) In her prayer texts, she declares that her very nature is fire. Clothed in the fire of charity, burning with desire to love and serve her neighbor gratuitously and to respond to all requests for her presence, she moves from her quiet beginnings in the streets of Siena to the centers of world power where her voice is heard by the mighty who respect the humble. Hardship and criticism do not deter her. Ever restless for the final union of death, she lives out her life in peaceful harmony; all her powers function as one:

> All their senses make one sweet sound, which comes forth from the center of the city of the soul. . . . The soul's movements, then, make a jubilant sound, its chords tempered and harmonized with prudence and light, all of them melting into one sound, the glorification and praise of my name. (D. 147:310)

ENDNOTES

1. Psychology validates the importance for mental health of the integration of the inner experience of the mystic with outer reality, of contemplation and action, of love of God and love of neighbor. "The mystic's life may be seen as a recognition of the existence of the inner, personal experience, which though independent of, and even antagonistic to, the social reality, cannot be fully developed unless the individual also affirms his/her role in society. Beautiful and powerful feelings are not sufficient. . . . What is needed is the integration of these inner experiences with the various social roles one adopts." Kenneth Wapnik, "Mysticism and Schizophrenia," *Journal of Transpersonal Psychology*, I (1969, 2), pp. 65-66.

2. Though no record survives to document the meeting, the convergence of the three major personages involved and the outcome, Raymond's appointment as Catherine's official confessor, suggest that an agreement was reached by the highest authority of the Dominican Order to override local authority. When Raymond recorded his activities a month later, he was in Siena, acting as Catherine's confessor, and it was clear that a relationship had developed between them. (L. 222-232) Two years later, in 1376, Pope Gregory XI issued a Papal Bull, which does survive, in which he referred to the decision made by Elias of Toulouse in 1374, repeated it, and confirmed its content. The papal document stated that Raymond of Capua would assume responsibility not only for Catherine, but also for the Mantellate who were Catherine's followers, indicating a break with the Sienese sisters and the friars who had wished to have her silenced and reprimanded. Raymond did not clarify the manner of the resolution of Catherine's early conflicts beyond recording that "she herself chose me as her confessor," and that he "defied those who objected to her frequent reception of communion" and "did all I could to satisfy her in this matter." (L. 284) Kearns, *Life of Catherine of Siena*, Intro., pp. xvi-xvii; Noffke, *Dialogue*, Intro., p. 5. For the most recent scholarship in this question, both are in debt to Timoteo M. Centi, O.P., "Un processo inventato di sana pianta," *Rassegna di Ascetica e Mystica*, XXI (1970), pp. 325-342.

3. *Letters*, 20, p. 81.
4. An important contribution to Catherine's peace of mind was the opportunity to discuss, and thereby come to understand, the meaning of her visions with a person well grounded in theology. Since medieval women were not formally educated, a reliable theologian/confessor was essential to her spiritual well-being; frequently in this interchange the woman became as much teacher of divine truth as student. See Petroff, p. 54, 57; Bynum, *Holy Feast*, pp. 22-23.
5. *I, Catherine*, Letter 35, p. 160.
6. Ibid., Letter 46, p. 203.
7. Ibid., Letter 39, p. 177.
8. Ibid., Letter 38, p. 169.
9. Ibid., Letter 60b, pp. 274-275.
10. Ibid., Letter 42, p. 189.
11. Ibid., Letter 44, p. 197.
12. *Letters*, 70, p. 219.
13. *I, Catherine*, Letter 38, p. 170. In this letter Catherine reveals that Saint Paul is one source of her clothing symbolism. "The sweet herald Paul did just this, for he put on Christ crucified and was stripped of his joy in the divine Essence. He puts on Christ the man, that is, the sufferings and opprobrium of Christ crucified; indeed he seeks to glory in nothing else, saying: 'Far be it from me to glory in anything but the cross of Christ crucified'. And in this the apostle found such joy that, as he himself once told his servant [Catherine, in a vision] 'Dearest child, I fastened that joy so tightly with the thong of love and desire that I was never stripped of it nor was it even loosened until life itself was taken from me.' "
14. Ibid., Letter 53, p. 233.
15. Ibid., Letter 55, p. 240.
16. Ibid., Letter 56, p. 243.
17. Ibid., Letter 40, p. 180.
18. Ibid., Letter 32, p. 147.
19. Ibid., Letter 55, p. 240.
20. Ibid., Letter 55, p. 242.
21. This visit to Pisa undoubtedly gave Catherine her first view of the sea, which had figured so forcefully in her concept of being immersed in the Godhead. From Pisa, Catherine wrote to Bartolomeo Dominici, "I invite you to enter into a calm deep sea. I have just discovered this again — not that the sea is new, though it is new to me, as I feel it in my soul — in the words: 'God is love.' " *Letters*, 27, p. 98.
22. John 14:6.
23. Ibid.
24. *Letters*, 61, p. 194.
25. Ibid., 28, p. 100.
26. Ibid., 53, p. 164.
27. Ibid., 59, p. 186.
28. Ibid., 2, p. 42.
29. *I, Catherine*, Letter 55, p. 239.
30. Ibid., p. 240.
31. *Letters*, 31, p. 108.
32. Ibid., 34, p. 118.
33. Ibid., 38, p. 127.
34. Ibid., 86, pp. 261-262.

PART THREE

MY NATURE IS FIRE:
THE PUBLIC FIGURE

Any society desiring to overcome its own violence, self-interest, and cynicism has need of mystic prayer since its essential components — persistence, intensity, and an "absolutely pure and genuine emotional feeling" — enhance both an understanding of God and of each other.[1] The Conference of American Catholic Bishops recognized this need in its 1983 pastoral statement "The Challenge of Peace":

> The practice of contemplative prayer is especially valuable for advancing harmony and peace in the world. For this prayer rises, by divine grace, where there is total disarmament of the heart and unfolds in an experience of love which is the moving force of peace. Contemplation fosters a vision of the human family as united and interdependent in the mystery of God's love for all people. This silent interior prayer bridges temporarily the "already" and "not yet," this world and God's kingdom of peace.[2]

As a child of six, Catherine was incapable of this type of prayer; however, mature love brought her to a relationship that fostered this mystic level of prayer, one that is capable of releasing the most powerful energy in the universe, "an energy that can build the earth and carry forward the thrust of evolution."[3]

Reaching to the very core of Godhead and finding herself

reflected in the mirror of a compassionate God, Catherine becomes absorbed in reflecting that presence to her world with an energy and an empathy, both encompassing and passionate, that will endure for the remainder of her life. Submerged in the fire of divine charity — a coal burning with the intensity of the whole fire — Catherine discovers the inseparable unity between a prayer that addresses God and a prayer that addresses her neighbor. The needs of the Church and of God's people stimulate Catherine to a prayer of petition that begs God continuously to have mercy for the world. At the same time, example and teaching, advising and admonishing, are the options given her to "share the fruits" of her vineyard in a hungry longing for peace.

In several instances, Catherine clearly states her perception of God's call to service. With her customary mix of simplicity and profundity, she writes to Raymond and other disciples early in 1376 of her resolution "to devote myself solely to seeking God's honor, the salvation of souls, and the renewal and exaltation of holy Church; and, by the grace and strength of the Holy Spirit, to persevere until death."[4] Later in the same year, she restates her mission in a letter to Pope Gregory XI: "My one desire in this life is to see God honored, your peace restored, holy Church reformed and the life of grace in every rational creature."[5] In the *Dialogue,* God's voice gives further testimony to this understanding:

> Make it your concern, then, to offer prayers for all people and for the mystic body of holy Church and for those I have given you to love with a special love. Do not be guilty of indifference about offering prayers and the example of your living and the word or your teaching. Reprove vice and commend virtue. Do all this to the greatest extent of your power. (D. 109:204)

In every circumstance in which she found herself, Catherine addressed these goals. Though never indifferent to vice and virtue, rarely did she seek out public causes; either they were near at hand, demanding her charity, or she addressed them because of the urgent petition of others. Whether responding to the needy of her own neighborhood, to the victims of the plague epidemic of 1374, or to the resolution of violent and vengeful family conflicts, Catherine sought to alleviate suffering and to restore right relationships, both between and among individuals and between humans and their God.

Drawn into the search for peace in Italy as mediator between the Tuscan cities and the papal authorities, Catherine's perceptive understanding of human nature led her to look beyond the disobedience of unruly subjects to the root causes of dissension and discord: poor administration in Italy, absentee government, self-centered churchmen, and a personally weak and vacillating pontiff. She targeted the basis for resolving these dilemmas in the change of the hearts and minds of people who were rightly invested with authority and responsibility to resolve crises and bring peace.

The following chapter details one episode in Catherine's public activity to demonstrate her adherence to her own principles of direction: her use of letter writing to effect change in her society, and her exposition of the principles and practices of good government as understood in the climate of her day. A group of letters to Pope Gregory XI commence in January of 1376 when he was in Avignon and continue until his arrival in Rome early in 1377. These letters permit analysis of the scope of her work and provide tangible evidence of Catherine's work as a seeker of justice and maker of peace in a violent time and place.

Catherine's directives comment on the personal requirements placed on the Pope as well as the relationship between papal governance, justice, and peace. The strong parallels between Catherine's ideas on these issues and those represented in the Lorenzetti cycle of frescoes on Good and Bad Government, detailed in Chapter One, underscore both the relevance of the paintings in medieval thought and their formative influence on Catherine's perception of justice and peace.

In the final chapter, Catherine's prayer texts permit entry into her perception of her relationship with God as well as the wide-ranging content of her petitionary prayer. Though denied access to her prayer of silence — by its very nature impossible to record — the available texts allow the privilege and the opportunity to pray with this medieval woman.

ENDNOTES

1. Nicoll, pp. 84, 88.
2. Pastoral Statement of the U.S. Conference of Catholic Bishops, Saint Paul Editions, Boston, 1983, p. 72.
3. Johnston, *Silent Music*, p. 174.
4. *I, Catherine*, Letter 21, p. 116.
5. Ibid., Letter 29, pp. 140-141.

8

ADVISING AND ADMONISHING:
A HUNGRY LONGING FOR PEACE

Catherine rooted her obedience and her loving dedication to the Church in an absolute conviction of the Trinitarian nature of that Church as bride of the Father, treasury of the redemptive blood of the Son, and dwelling place of the Spirit. The continued assertion of this concept in Catherine's writings testifies to its centrality in her thinking. She states succinctly in her prayer, "and you have stored this blood in the wine cellar of holy Church, giving the keys and the guardianship of it to your chief vicar on earth." (P. 24:208) "Sweet Christ on earth," the vicar of Christ, the supreme pontiff, the cellarer who held the keys to the wine cellar, had the responsibility to administer the blood and to delegate ministers to help him.

The papal power of appointment over the ministers of the Church implied both the right and the responsibility to admonish and to correct those who failed in their duty. Whenever papal appointees abused their privileged positions, either in religious or political matters, all of society suffered. True justice required virtue not only in Church leaders and Church administration but also in the governed; each side of this issue claimed Catherine's energy. Thus, in the third petition of the *Dialogue*, she prayed for the Christians who had rebelled against the Church, a tacit recognition that they were victims of injustice. (D. 1:26) This was the vantage point from which Catherine addressed the cause of peace in her day, "with a hungry longing for peace,"[1] a peace that would reign when justice flowed from a proper exercise of and from a respect for authority.

Catherine's initial contact with Gregory had come in March of 1374, the fourth year of Gregory's pontificate and a few months before Catherine received the official affirmation and protection of the Dominican Order. Interestingly enough, Gregory communicated with her almost immediately following the death of another influential mystic on whom he had relied, Birgitta of Sweden.[2] In a letter to her Dominican disciple, Bartolomeo Dominici, Catherine recorded, "the pope sent his representative here, the one who was spiritual father to that countess who died in Rome," continuing, "he came to me in the holy father's name to say that I should offer special prayer for him and for holy Church."[3] Since history frequently generalizes the efforts of holy women like Catherine and Birgitta of Sweden as self-appointed attempts to influence the pope according to their own perceptions of right and wrong, Catherine's reference to Gregory's early overture to her is significant. It indicates both the papal initiative in their relationship and Gregory's penchant to be associated with and his need to be confirmed by "holy persons."

Catherine's interactions with Gregory XI range over a variety of issues, but three predominate in her letters to him: peace in Italy, the return of the papal seat to Rome, and the calling of a crusade to pacify the Holy Land and to convert the non-Christian peoples of the near East. The first two, in her judgment, were inextricably linked and of primary significance for the well-being of the Church. The third would solidify the peace of Europe by distracting warring elements on the continent and enrich the Church by the addition of new converts.

In Catherine's world, the condition of the Church, both political and spiritual, was of overriding significance to all people whose public and private lives were intimately affected by its power and influence. This was especially true in fourteenth century Italy where the Avignon Papacy, in an effort to organize

its administrative structure, had created a cadre of French appointees to rule in the territories directly controlled by the
Church. Accompanying the hated imposition of foreign rulers was
an acknowledged profiteering by papal appointees; this abuse
further agitated the precarious balance of peace in the Italian
peninsula. [4]

Papal control over Italy intensified in the opening years of
the reign of Gregory XI as a preliminary step in the return of the
papal administrative center to Rome. A concerted effort at pacification and occupation included the formation of a papal league in
1371 to secure the support and/or neutrality of a network of
independent Italian cities and petty kingdoms; the hiring of
mercenaries like the infamous John Hawkwood to subjugate restless rivals; the occupation by papal forces of the city of Perugia;
and the appointment of papal vicars to rule the smaller Italian
communes. After the pacification of the rebellious Visconti family
in Milan, following Gregory's threat to preach a crusade against
them, the Italian peninsula began to resemble a papal kingdom. [5]

Florence, Siena, and Pisa, having refrained from joining the
papal league, observed their growing encirclement with concern.
Florentines, who had long cherished the ambition to dominate all
of Tuscany, not only saw this hope dissipating in the face of a new
exertion of papal strength, but began to fear the loss of independence. Florence, therefore, called for an anti-papal league in July of
1375 and exerted pressure on neighboring cities and towns to join
them. In December of that year, encouraged by Florentine agita-
tion, a wave of revolts swept Italy until the Church lost its
precarious control so recently extended over the Italian posses-
sions. Gregory responded to the increase in hostilities by placing
Florence under interdict, calling upon all European monarchs to
expel Florentine merchants from their midst and to confiscate
their property.

From the very beginning of hostilities, Catherine was deeply
concerned by all these incidents. Her incursion into the world of

international diplomacy reveals her astute understanding of the medieval scheme of power. Catherine's letters to Queen Giovanna of Naples, to the Queen Mother of Hungary, and to the mercenary John Hawkwood have the purpose of cementing and confirming the bonds of the papal league and of seeking support for a projected crusade.[6] Similarly, letters to the Visconti, to the rulers of Bologna, Perugia, Lucca, and Pisa call them to their duties as Christians in the fellowship of the Church,[7] while her letters to the Pope call him to his duty to preserve the peace.[8]

Soon, Catherine was drawn more directly into the widening conflict. Florentines, wishing to keep channels of communication open, decided to make use of intermediaries favored by Gregory. Since Catherine was the pre-eminent religious personage in Tuscany, they decided toward the end of March to send as emissaries to Avignon a small group of her followers, led by Raymond.[9] Shortly after their departure, Catherine, on the first of April, had the prayer experience related earlier in which she felt Christ place a cross on her shoulders and an olive branch in her hands, and understood that she must "carry it to the Christians and unbelievers alike."[10] This experience drew her directly into the political situation. Following it, she offered her services to the Republic of Florence, and in the semi-formal capacity of peace negotiator, she went directly to the papal court.

Like the simplest of medieval persons, Pope Gregory XI was drawn to seek advice from reputed holy people. Catherine's written responses to his messages indicate that the Pope often requested her prayers,[11] asked her advice about the timing of his return to Rome,[12] and seemed to seek predictions regarding his safety during and after the journey.[13] Gregory was not a corrupt man; rather, he was one placed in a situation of historic proportions. Made cardinal by his uncle, Pope Clement VI, at the age of nineteen, he was forty-two when elected to the papal throne. Renowned among his subordinates for prudence and discretion, for personal piety, goodness, and uprightness of character, Gregory was generous in support of religious undertakings, zealous for the reform of religious orders, and active in promoting peace between warring nation-states. However, he tolerated the continuance of an atmosphere at Avignon and in Church government in which pleasure, luxury, and easy moral standards prevailed. [14]

Catherine's letters reveal that even before she was actively drawn into the Florentine papal dispute, she was well-informed both about the personality of the Pope and about international events. A year after Gregory had made contact with her, Catherine responded to questions raised in a letter from the Papal Nuncio in Tuscany, Berengario, in which she indicated both the Pope's personal failings and their public consequences. His excessive attachment to and concern for his relatives together with his weakness and leniency in the correction of his subordinates permitted the rule of unworthy, evil, and rapacious men appointed to office because of "flattery, money, or simony." [15] These appointees, she indicated, were destructive of good government in the Church. [16]

Catherine's habitual custom, to seek the reformation of the individual person as the surest means to effect radical change in society as a whole, held true in her dealings with the Pope. The cause of peace demanded Gregory's personal reformation. Like the ruler in the Allegory of Good Government, he must acquire the requisite virtues, root out vice in himself, and demand high standards from those who rule under him. Invested with authority, he has the responsibility to use it to eradicate the evils which cause social injustice and lead citizens into rebellion against the Church.

In her opening letter to Gregory, Catherine introduces her foundational symbol of the fruitful tree set in the soil of self-knowledge. A productive tree, one which will be laden with fruit, must be set in the soil of self-knowledge, she declares, while a tree, uprooted from this soil, will dry up and bear no fruit. [17] According to Catherine, self-knowledge generates humility, and humble people see no reason for pride since charity teaches them about God's boundless goodness and their own nothingness. In contrast, pride, the opposite of humility, is a worm of self-love gnawing away at the root of the tree, rendering it barren of fruit, even of the virtue necessary to bring forth this fruit of praise and glory to God's name.

Though Catherine does not accuse Gregory of personal immorality, she designates vainglory as his prevailing vice. "Evil pride" and "self- centeredness," the "head and origin of all evil," kill "holy justice" in a ruler and permit the reign of avarice and tyranny in his subordinates. She reminds him that the virtue that is so necessary for the ordinary person is even more important in one who must govern holy Church.[18] Even a prelate, Catherine warns Gregory, can act out of self-love and promote injustice when he fears to offend and make enemies, when he pretends not to see and, therefore, fails to correct wrongdoing in his subordinates. This is why your subjects are corrupt, full of impurity and iniquity, she declares.[19]

Self-love induces cowardice; in Gregory, this trait is characterized as a lack of determination which permits others to frighten him with threats of personal danger.[20] "Nothing," Catherine warns, "thwarts God's honor and the reform and advancement of holy Church" as much as fear.[21] Her exhortations multiply: be a courageous man and not a coward;[22] confront danger like a brave man with strength, patience, and enduring perseverance;[23] grow from slavish fear to holy fear.[24] Her prayers for Gregory center on firmness, stability, strength, and patience,[25] symbolized in the solidity of a rock of determination and resolution.[26] Finally, her warnings against cowardice lead to an examination of his exercise of authority.

In Catherine's vision of things, the papal responsibility to appoint and correct the ministers of the Church is of extreme importance; failure to exercise this right with courage and conviction makes the pontiff accountable both for the conduct of his

appointees and for the evil effects that unworthy clerics produce
in the government of the Church. In the *Dialogue*, she refers to
examples in the past, when the Church was a strong and forceful
presence in society, when popes properly exercised this duty in
justice:

> The pearl of justice shone in them and in their subjects, but
> first of all in them, . . . Because they had first done justice to
> themselves, they were just to their subjects as well . . .
> They wanted them to live virtuously, and so they corrected
> them without any slavish fear, for their concern was not for
> themselves but only for my honor and the salvation of souls.
> They conducted themselves as good shepherds and follow-
> ers of the good shepherd, my Truth. (D. 119:223)

Among the churchmen of her own day, Catherine charges
that the neglect of this guiding corrective authority is based on
fear of losing their rank and position and their material posses-
sions. She labels it "injustice" when leaders fail to correct evil
done by their subjects, or when they pretend not to see or fear to
correct. (D. 119:224) In Gregory, over-attachment to and over-
concern about relatives — also rooted in self-love — manifest
themselves in his neglect to discipline Church ministers.
Catherine insists this tendency be curbed for "nothing else will
hinder your good holy desire or thwart God's honor and the
reform and advancement of holy Church" as much as this. [27]

Catherine's language matches the strength of her conviction
as she calls Gregory to his duty. One who accepts authority
incurs the responsibility to use it diligently, to rebuke evil, and to
correct those under him. [28] "If you don't intend to use it," she
states, "it would be better and more to God's honor and the good
of your soul to resign."[29] Using the spiritual prestige that, in her,
flows from inner power, Catherine models for Gregory the
proper use of his authority to correct evil where it exists. She
warns him that if he fails to exercise his responsibility, he will be

severely rebuked by God, adding, "If I were in your place I would be afraid of incurring divine judgment."

Instead of the Prudence, Fortitude, Magnanimity, and Temperance which promote good government, Catherine indicates the presence of the opposing vices of bad government both in the Church and in territorial administration. Tyranny, Avarice, and Vainglory reign among Gregory's churchmen and inspire Cruelty, Perfidy, Fraud, and Anger. Her litany of vice and abuse is repeated over and over: pride, greed, and avarice; worldly luxury, ambition, pretentious vanity, love of one's own status, honor and pleasure; concern for wealth, food, elegant houses, and fine horses.[30] Failure to appoint men of high caliber to administrative office cripples "the common good of the Christian congregation and the reform of holy Church."[31]

Gregory's leniency allows the weeds of impurity, avarice, and pride to flourish in the garden of holy Church.[32] His appointments are made, not because of the virtue and the capability of the appointee but because of flattery, pride, and financial gain. No wonder that his subjects rise up against him! As ardent a lover and supporter of the Church as she is, Catherine cannot ignore the fact that much of the disobedience and anti-papal spirit in Italy is initiated by policies promulgated in the name of the Church by unworthy leaders. People have suffered such injustice, inequity, and unfairness, Catherine declares, that they have no alternative but to revolt.[33] Like the justice in chains in the Allegory of Bad Government, Justice cannot prevail where vice is permitted to predominate in administrators. Injustice breeds discord and war; bad leaders provoke rebellion.[34]

Since justice requires the reward of the good and the punishment of the wrongdoer, Catherine allows that Gregory cannot permit the misdeeds of his subjects to go unpunished; strict justice requires that he exact vengeance.[35] "Punish the criminal and exact whatever each can yield," she directs. However, the justice of a spiritual leader must be tempered with mercy and charity. [36] "Receive your subjects with magnanimity despite their persecution and injustice," Catherine advises, calling Gregory to his role as pontiff, father, and good shepherd. [37] "Use your kindness to conquer their malice," she pleads, promising Gregory that if he acts gently, "they will all come and lay their heads in your lap in sorrow for what they have done." [38] She tells him they await a conciliatory sign. [39]

As in the Allegory, so, too, in Catherine's exposition, the proper administration of justice will bring peace to Gregory's domain. Lorenzetti's painting shows Sienese citizens paying their just taxes and tributes, acknowledging proper dominion over lands and castles, all without war, because when justice prevails, peace and concord follow. Catherine holds out this prospect to Gregory. Peace is her overall objective. "Make peace with all of Tuscany," she pleads. "You can see that justice is done; you can have peace. . . . You have the authority to give peace to those who ask you." [40] "Re-establish peace," she urges. [41] Become an instrument and means of bringing peace to the world by using "your power and authority diligently and with a hungry longing for peace." [42] "I beg you," she writes, "to invite those who have rebelled against you to a holy peace . . ." [43] You will emerge from war into the greatest peace, from persecution to unity by means of virtue. [44] Repeatedly, there is the refrain, "Peace, peace, peace, no more war!" [45]

Though her language grows severe at times, Catherine always encourages this hesitant and sensitive pontiff, deferring to him as Christ's human representative in the Church. "If 'til now you haven't been very firm in the truth, I want you, I beg you, for the little time there is left, to be so," she writes. "And don't be afraid . . . attend to spiritual affairs, to appointing good pastors and administrators in your cities for you have experienced rebellion because of bad pastors and administrators." [46]

It was as much the influence of the licentious character of the Avignon papal court as the deleterious effect on civic and political conditions in Italy that made Catherine so insistent on a return of the papal court to Rome. "Come," she wrote, "don't resist any longer the will of God who is calling you . . . come and take possession of the place of your predecessor and model, the apostle Peter. You as Christ's vicar, ought to be residing in your proper place."[47]

Catherine's words place her securely within the context of the political realities of her day, an intellectual framework demonstrated both in the pictorial images of the Lorenzetti triad of frescoes and in the medieval thinking which these paintings represent. She speaks in a medieval language, a language understood and valued by her contemporaries, a language rooted in commonly held medieval concepts of virtue, justice, and peace as requisite components of good government. Speaking with conviction, acting with dignity, conscious of her power, its source, and her own responsibility to use it for the common good, Catherine is aware of her unusual position. However, she makes no apologies for her gender, only for her boldness in addressing such a lofty personage.

In a papal court known for its splendor and extravagances, this young woman, simply dressed and speaking an unintelligible dialect, was an imposing and credible presence. That she was heard by honest people is proof of the truth of her perception of the court and the condition of the Church; that she was feared by those who resisted reform and change of location signified the seriousness of the threat she represented. When the Avignon circle produced a letter, reputed to be from another holy seer, warning Gregory that death awaited him on his return to Rome, Catherine mercilessly exposed it as a falsehood.[48] She addressed letters to military leaders in the Italian provinces winning pledges either of active support or of non-intervention. Consequently, mercenaries and leaders with military interests were drawn to the cause of a crusade, her long-standing and passionate desire.

The dictums she addressed to the Pope were disarming in

their simplicity but radical in their gospel foundation. The peace
that Catherine urged on Gregory was that of a good shepherd
who went in search of sheep who were lost. Finding them, such a
shepherd did not respond in anger and war as a solution nor even
mete out deserved punishment. Her directives contain the essence of true peace which begins in the heart of an individual,
especially one who holds the balance between war and peace
within his authoritative power.

Gregory's troubled passage from Avignon to Rome was
finally underway when Catherine returned to the symbolism of
the fruitful tree:

> I want you to be a tree of love grafted into Love the Word,
> Christ crucified . . . In the midst of your sufferings you will
> find peace, serenity and consolation when you see that by
> suffering you are being conformed to Christ crucified. By
> thus enduring with him, you will come joyfully from great
> war to great peace. [49]

However, the end to war still eluded Catherine. The timid
Pope was further terrorized on his return to a city physically
deteriorated and torn by violence during the long papal exile.
Catherine herself had yet to face the angry mobs of the city of
Florence in her tireless quest for peace for that city which would
not be finalized until after Gregory's death. Reform within the
Church was delayed and problems were compounded by the
schismatic election of a second Pope following Urban VI's succes-
sion to Gregory. None of these setbacks deterred Catherine's
efforts for the Church.

She continued to offer herself, her mind and body, her
strength and weakness, her prayer and her pen for the welfare of
the Church. Two months before her death, she wrote to
Raymond and recounted her final offering of herself:

> O Eternal God, receive the sacrifice of my life into this
> mystical body of holy Church. I have nothing to give except

what you have given me so take my heart and squeeze it out over the face of the Bride. [50]

In this, her last written communication to Raymond, Catherine revealed the indomitable hope eternally rising in the breast of one who had total trust, not in her own strength but in him who strengthened her:

> Thanks, thanks to be to the most high eternal God, who has placed us as knights on the battlefield to do combat for his Bride with the shield of most holy faith. The field is ours. The very power and might that defeated the demon who had mankind in his grip . . . shall again work his ruin; that is, he will be defeated, not by what our bodies suffer, but by virtues of the glowing measureless Charity of God. [51]

Catherine saw in the Church a human reflection of God's love for his creatures, a love immeasurable enough to allow Christ to die ignominiously to save them. Catherine longed to die for the Church, to offer her life for its deliverance from the travail which she witnessed. Her final days were passed in an agony of love for the mystic bride, holy Church.

ENDNOTES

1. *Letters*, 63, p. 201.
2. Birgitta of Sweden (1303-1373) is often paired with Catherine in discussion of the papal return to Rome and the general moral reform of the Church. Like Catherine she was a mystic whose prayer life generated activity for the good of the Church; she lived in Rome from 1349-1373.
3. *Letters*, 20, p. 81.
4. Guillaume Mollat, *The Popes at Avignon, 1305-1378*, Thomas Nelson and Sons, London, 1963, p. 165. Mollat observes, "It is only too true that many of these Frenchmen regarded Italy merely as a place where they could rapidly amass a fortune. . . . The Vatican registers . . . prove how well founded were the complaints of the populations of the Italian cities."
5. Ibid., p. 161.

6. *Letters*, 30, p. 105; 32, p. 111; 39, p. 128; 40, p. 130; 41, p. 134.
7. Ibid., 17, p. 67; 18, p. 72; 53, p. 162; 60, p. 187; 68, p. 212; 72, p. 223.
8. Ibid., 54, p. 166; 63, p. 200; 64, p. 203.
9. Ibid., 63, pp. 200-203. Raymond carried a letter of credential from Catherine to Gregory.
10. Ibid., 65, p. 207.
11. Ibid., 76, p. 235; 80, p. 244.
12. Ibid., 69, p. 218.
13. Ibid., 76, p. 235.
14. Mollat, pp. 59-62.
15. *Letters*, 51, p. 156.
16. On December 21, 1375, Gregory created nine new Cardinals; the quality of his choices destroyed any hope for reform in the College of Cardinals. Edmund G. Gardner, *Saint Catherine of Siena: A Study in the Religion, Literature and History of the Fourteenth Century in Italy*, E.P. Dutton, New York, 1907, p. 15. In a letter to Gregory Catherine commented, "I believe it would be to God's honor and better for you to be careful always to choose virtuous men. Otherwise it will be a great insult to God and disastrous to holy Church. And then let's not be surprised if God sends us his chastening scourges, and justly." Ibid., 54, p. 169.
17. Ibid., 54, p. 166.
18. Ibid., 88, p. 265.
19. Ibid., 54, p. 166.
20. Ibid., 76, p. 234.
21. Ibid., 71, p. 222.
22. Ibid., 63, p. 202.
23. Ibid., 88, p. 266.
24. Ibid., 76, p. 234.
25. Ibid., 88, p. 264.
26. Ibid., 77, pp. 235-236.
27. Ibid., 71, p. 222.
28. Ibid., 63, p. 201.
29. Ibid., 71, p. 222.
30. Ibid., 63, p. 201; 74, p. 230; 77, p. 236.
31. Ibid., 81, p. 246.
32. Ibid., 63, p. 201.
33. Ibid., 64, p. 205.
34. Ibid., 54, p. 169.
35. Ibid., 64, p. 204.
36. Ibid., 64, p. 204; 71, p. 222.
37. Ibid., 74, p. 229.
38. Ibid., 54, pp. 167-168; 64, pp. 204-205; 74, pp. 229-230.
39. Ibid., 64, p. 205.
40. Ibid., 71, pp. 222-223.
41. Ibid., 74, p. 229.
42. Ibid., 63, p. 201.
43. Ibid., 54, p. 169.
44. Ibid., 63, p. 202.
45. Ibid., 74, p. 231; 88, p. 266.
46. Ibid., 54, p. 169.

47. Ibid., 64, p. 205.
48. Ibid., 81, pp. 245-247.
49. Ibid., 88, p. 166.
50. *I, Catherine*, Letter 60b, p. 276.
51. Ibid., pp. 276-277.

9

HOLY AND CONSTANT PRAYER: MERCY FOR THE WORLD

As with each individual, Catherine of Siena expresses her own inner reality in her prayer. Thus, to meet Catherine's God is to discover the secret of her own nature, spoken in the naked intimacy of creature to Creator. Images of God flow from her fertile imagination to surface from her unconscious depths words which name and identify her experience.[1] These images reveal the Godhead into which she has entered so fully that in the *Dialogue* God states, "And if anyone should ask me what this soul is, I would say: She is another me, made so by the union of love." (D. 96:181)

Hers is a God who is "mad with love," "drunk with love," descriptive phrases which she applies to both God and herself in her own spontaneous prayer from the *Dialogue*:

> O mad lover! And you have need of your creature? It seems so to me, for you act as if you could not live without her, in spite of the fact that you are life itself, and everything has life from you and nothing can have life without you. Why then are you so mad? Because you have fallen in love with what you have made! You are pleased and delighted over her within yourself, as if you were drunk with desire for her salvation. She runs away from you and you go looking for her. She strays and you draw closer to her. (D. 153:325)

As would be expected, her God expresses the harmony that is the goal of all her spiritual striving. Catherine encounters Godhead, the wellspring, the unified totality of all that is. Within the Godhead, *Deità*, she meets the three Persons of the Trinity, so crucial to her conception of the human imaging of triune Oneness by means of the memory, understanding, and will. She habitually attributed to these Persons power, wisdom, and mercy. However, this was but one facet of her conception of their Personhood; streams of salutations flowed in her prayer: unutterable love, infinite goodness, purest beauty, peaceful sea, fire always burning, immense fire and affection of charity, food, life, wisdom, and light, with each imaged repetitively, many interchangeably.

Unlike Julian of Norwich, Catherine did not discover a mother God within her being. Transcending delineations of gender differences, mothering was one among many divine manifestations; the kindness, nurturance, mercy, the ability to feed a child, tenderness, and sweetness that characterized Julian's mother God are also manifested in Catherine's *Deità*, but neither as masculine nor feminine. [2] Her consistent qualities overlap the distinctions of persons forming a picture of Catherine's enduring perception of her God and of the qualities she valued and strove to achieve in her mirrored likeness.

Compassion, love, goodness, mercy, tenderness, gentleness, truth, and charity — here is a word picture of the natural self Catherine seeks within. The opposite poles of these qualities confirm the existence of another side of Catherine which she continually struggles to bring into balanced harmony, the part of her that is, by nature, passionate and fiery. Because of this nature, love dominates her presentation of the divine. "It was with providence that I created you, and when I contemplated my creature in myself I fell in love with the beauty of my creation." (D. 135:277)

Her sense of her own image reflected in the mirror of God is captured most strikingly in this description of herself:

In your nature
eternal Godhead,
I shall come to know my nature.
And what is my nature, boundless love?
It is fire,
because you are nothing but a fire of love.
And you have given humankind
a share in this nature
for by the fire of love
you created us.
(P. 12:104)

Catherine discovers her own nature of fire in the reflection of the divinity; she imaged final union as a coal immersed in fire, fused into the fire itself, into the "blazing furnace of charity." The profundity of this identification emerges as we study her perception of God as fire; here, she addresses the Trinity:

O fire ever burning
fire that never goes out,
never dims,
never can be diminished
even if the whole world takes fire from you!
(P. 20:186)

Christ's passion is the fire of charity brought to perfect fulfillment:

For then the fire
hidden under our ashes
began to show itself
completely and generously
by splitting open his
most holy body
on the wood of the cross.
And it was to draw the soul's affection
to high things,

> and to bring the mind's eye
> to gaze into the fire,
> that your eternal Word
> wanted to be lifted up high.
> (P. 19:172)

Catherine's writings return continually to this image. In the *Dialogue*, we sense the pulsing refrain of the sequence of Pentecost:

> You are a fire always burning but never consuming; you are
> a fire consuming in your heat all the soul's selfish love; you
> are a fire lifting all chill and giving light. (D. 167:365)

In a letter, she advises a follower to become wood consumed in the sweet fire of God's love:

> He can only become one with fire by throwing himself right
> in and being completely enveloped in it . . . Once a man, thus
> bound, is enveloped in the fire of divine Charity, it produces
> in his soul the effects of material fire, which gives heat and
> light and transforms everything into itself . . . The heat
> warms and sets alight the dry wood of our will which then
> bursts into flame and expands with sweet and loving de-
> sire. . . .[3]

Catherine's prayer reveals her keen understanding of her place in the human/divine relationship, her clear distinction between the divine nature and her human nature; this was an early lesson taught her by Christ. She prayed:

> In your light I see
> and without it I cannot see,
> for you are the one who is
> and I am the one who is not.
> (P. 20:186)

This understanding confirms Catherine's hold on a sincere and genuine purification of emotions, the recognition of who she is and who God is, a requisite attitude for the prayer that will "connect" with the higher level of divinity:[4]

> But if I gaze into your exaltedness,
> any rising up to there
> that my soul can manage
> is as the dark night
> compared with the light of the sun,
> or as different as is the moonlight
> from the sun's globe.
> For I, mortal lowliness,
> cannot reach up to your immortal greatness.
> True,
> I can experience you
> through love's affection,
> but I cannot see you as you really are. . . .
> It is very true then
> that my lowliness
> cannot reach up to your exaltedness,
> but can only see and experience you
> in your mirror,
> and this by becoming perfect in charity.
> (P. 19:170-171)

Her total dependence as creature, despite her resemblance to her Creator, is foremost in her mind as she approaches God in prayer, seeing in herself God's image and likeness:

> You, eternal God,
> saw me and knew me
> in yourself.
> And because you saw me in your light
> you fell in love with your creature
> and drew her out of yourself
> and created her in your image and likeness.

> But this did not make it possible
> for me your creature
> to know you in myself
> except as I saw in myself
> your image and likeness.
> (P. 13:108)

Fire, the image which Catherine chose to express her own nature, is likewise an image of Catherine's prayer as it expands to include not only personal relationship with God but also concern for the world around her. "Once we are in its embrace," she writes, "the fire of divine charity does to our soul what physical fire does: it warms us, enlightens us, changes us into itself. Oh gentle and fascinating fire! You warm and you drive out all the cold of vice and sin and self-centeredness!"[5] Catherine's prayer is filled with Christ's own desire, to renew the face of the earth.

Our Father, Hallowed Be Your Name

In the Our Father, presented by Jesus to his disciples as a model of prayer, all the elements required to bridge the lower and higher levels of the human and the divine are present.[6] Examining Catherine's prayer according to the elements of this model reveals her great wisdom and her command of the language of prayer. Each of her recorded prayers begins with an invocation of praise; some are multiple repetitions of the same words; others praise particular attributes governing a specific prayer. From her language, we deduce Catherine's recognition of her mortality, her understanding of the mysterious nature of the immortal God, and her clear intellectual perception of Whom she is addressing, the three distinct Persons of that mysterious oneness, Godhead, *Deità*. Some typical invocations follow:

Godhead!
Godhead!
Ineffable Godhead!
O supreme goodness
that for love alone made us in your image and likeness!
(P. 1:16)

Eternal Godhead!
O high eternal Godhead!
Boundless love!
In your light I have seen light;
in your light I have come to know the light.
(P. 11:87)

O eternal Trinity!
Eternal Trinity!
O fire and deep well of charity!
O you who are madly in love
with your creature!
O eternal truth!
O eternal fire!
O eternal wisdom
given for our redemption!
(P. 10:78)

Though the habitual quality she associates with the Father is power, the variety of attributes are unending: truth, tenderest love, divine compassion, boundless most gentle charity, love incomprehensible, gentle Lord, compassionate merciful Father, most gentle creator. Wisdom is her personification of the Son, but she also includes reconciler, refashioner, redeemer, priceless purity, most gentle love, spotless Lamb, truth, word, light, heavenly food, boundless love, cornerstone. The Spirit, characterized as gentle mercy, is also the love of the Father and Son, reason for creation, blazing charity, dew, fire, and deep well of charity. The degree to which Catherine's personal God is internalized in her being is seen in these explications of the Trinity. A characteristic prayer brings together Father, Son, and Spirit as power, wisdom, and mercy imaged in the three human powers of memory, understanding, and will:

> You,
> Godhead,
> one in being and three in Persons,
> are one vine with three branches —
> if I may be permitted to make such a comparison.
> You made us in your image and likeness so that,
> with our three powers in one soul,
> we might image your Trinity
> and your unity.
> And as we image,
> so we may find union:
> through our memory,
> image and be united with the Father,
> to whom is attributed power;
> through our understanding,
> image and be united with the Son,
> to whom is attributed wisdom;
> through our will,
> image and be united with the Holy Spirit,
> to whom is attributed mercy,
> and who is the love
> of the Father and Son.
> (P. 4:42)

In this prayer, Catherine uses the familiar phrase, "created in the image and likeness of God." As is her custom, she both extends and reverses the meaning of images. Here, she portrays human beings made in the image and likeness of God as well as imaging or mirroring the very unity and Trinity of the Godhead. She prays that "we might image your Trinity and your unity" in the three powers in one person. The use of image as a verb, coming from Catherine's use of the mirror symbolism is also familiar; in the *Dialogue*, she speaks of union as the mirror held in the hand of love which "shows me myself, as your creation, in you, and you in me through the union you have brought about of the Godhead with our humanity." (D. 167:366)

On the feast of the Annunciation, Catherine honors the Virgin Mary with a similar theme. Drawing on another allusion from the *Dialogue*, her being joined and kneaded in Christ's blood, she refers to Mary as "flour," and celebrates the merging of Godhead with human nature:

O Mary,
may you be proclaimed blessed among all women
for endless ages,
for today you have shared with us
your flour.
Today the Godhead
is joined and kneaded into one dough
with our humanity —
so securely
that this union could never be broken,
either by death
or by our thanklessness.
In fact,
the Godhead was united
even with Christ's body in the tomb
and with his soul in limbo,
and afterwards
with both his soul and body.
The relationship was so entered into
and sealed
that it will never be dissolved,
any more than it has been broken up until now.
(P. 18:164-165)

Catherine repeatedly returns to her recognition of oneness, not only that the three are one, but that each divine Person contains the whole of Godhead. This recognition can be seen in a prayer which opens with a triple invocation of the Son but continues with a deliberate explication of the inseparable presence of the three in the one Person of Christ:

> But did your wisdom come into the world alone?
> No.
> For wisdom is not separate from power,
> nor was power without mercy.
> Your wisdom did not come alone then,
> but the whole Trinity was there.
> (P. 10:78)

Similarly, she sees the Eucharist as containing the "whole of God":

> O fire of love!
> Was it not enough to gift us
> with creation in your image and likeness,
> and to create us anew to grace in your Son's blood,
> without giving us yourself as food,
> the whole of divine being,
> the whole of God?
> (P. 10:79)

In a prayer believed to be based on Jesus' Easter meeting with Mary Magdalene in the garden, Catherine combines these two principles: the human imaging of the Trinity in the three powers and the concept that the three Persons are always present in the one. This combination serves to heighten the meaning behind her insistence that "having climbed one stair, we have climbed them all"; the inseparable Persons of the Trinity mirror the inseparable powers and the inseparable stages of growth.

She situates herself in that place of meeting, absorbing each image in the garden:

> You are this matchless eternal garden,
> and you hold enclosed within yourself
> both the flowers and the fruits —
> for you are the flower of glory. . . .
> we were enclosed,
> O eternal Father,
> within the garden of your bosom.
> You drew us out of your holy mind
> like a flower
> petaled with our soul's three powers,
> and into each power
> you put the whole plant,
> so that they might bear fruit in your garden,
> might come back to you
> with the fruit you gave them.
> (P. 20:187-188)

The coming together of the three human powers into a unified oneness to mirror the Godhead, so central to the harmony Catherine seeks, finds expression in her image of the Trinity as table, food, and waiter. The mutuality of the Three and the unique expression of each one's loving care of her come to fruition in that outward burst of love and compassion that brings her to mirror their desire for the salvation of the whole world:[7]

> You, eternal Trinity,
> are table
> and food
> and waiter for us.
> You, eternal Father,
> are the table
> that offers us as food
> the Lamb, your only begotten Son.
> He is the most exquisite of foods for us,

both in his teaching,
which nourishes us in your will,
and in the sacrament
that we receive in holy communion,
which feeds and strengthens us
while we are pilgrim travelers in this life.
And the Holy Spirit
is indeed a waiter for us,
for he serves us this teaching
by enlightening our mind's eye with it
and inspiring us to follow it.
And he serves us charity for our neighbors
and hunger to have as our food
souls
for the salvation of the whole world
and for the Father's honor.
(P. 12:102)

Your Kingdom Come

That God's kingdom on earth prevail is the focus of Catherine's adult life! Close to the time when she began the *Dialogue,* she conceived the intention of offering her own self for the world, especially for the Church. The intensity of her dedication is seen in her prayer:

I have one body,
and to you I offer and return it.
Here is my flesh;
here is my blood;
let me be slain, reduced to nothing;
let my bones be split apart
for those for whom I am praying,
if such is your will.
(P. 1:20)

Her two concerns receive continuous reference:

> Give us a voice,
> your own voice,
> to cry out to you
> for mercy for the world
> and for the reform of holy Church.
> And listen to your own voice
> with which we cry out to you.
> (P. 10:80-81)

God's promise of mercy to the world is reiterated over and over again in the *Dialogue*, and the need for reform of God's Church is uppermost among the concerns it addresses. Catherine's conception of the Church and the role of the Pope are best seen through her image of Christ's blood as the means of salvation. The blood is stored in the wine cellar of holy Church and controlled by the cellarer, the keeper of the keys, the successor to Peter:

> You know I set before you the mystic body of holy Church under the image of a wine cellar. In this wine cellar was the blood of my only-begotten Son, and from this blood all the sacraments derive their life-giving power.
>
> Christ on earth the Pope stood at the door of this wine cellar. He had been commissioned to administer the blood, and it was his duty to delegate ministers to help him in the service of the entire universal body of Christianity. Only those accepted and anointed by him were to thus minister. He was the head of the whole clerical order, and he appointed each one to his proper office to administer this glorious blood. (D. 115:215)

In her prayer, we find the same theme:

By the power of this blood we are cleansed from sin
through your sacraments,
and you have stored this blood
in the wine cellar of holy Church,
giving the keys and guardianship of it
to your chief vicar on earth.
(P. 24:208)

Papal responsibility, the need for reform, and her willingness to sacrifice herself for the Church dominate much of Catherine's prayer:

Your vicar, then, surely ought to rejoice in doing your will
and following the justice of Christ Jesus,
who in his unutterable compassion for us
opened up and drained and let go of his most holy body,
and gave his blood
to wash our sins
and buy back our wholeness.
And he gave this vicar of yours the keys
for binding and freeing our souls,
so that he should do your will
and follow in his footsteps.
This is why I pray and beseech your most holy mercy
that you so purify him
that his heart may burn with holy desire
to win back your lost members, . . .
And if his dallying displeases you,
O love eternal,
punish my body for it,
for I offer and return it to you
to scourge and ravage as you please.
(P. 3:36-37)

Her concern for the Church and its vicar lead her to desire to give herself for its well-being:

Turn, merciful Father,
turn the eye of your compassion
on your bride
and on your vicar.
Hide him under the wings of your mercy
so that the wicked and the proud
may not harm him.
And grant me the grace to pour out my blood
and scatter the marrow of my bones
in this garden, holy Church.
(P. 15:132)

The clergy, the ministers of the Church, enter into her prayer as well:

I beg you to guide toward yourself
the heart and will of the ministers of holy Church, your bride,
so that they may follow you,
the slain Lamb,
poor, humble, and meek,
along the way of the most holy cross —
in your way, not their own.
Let them be angelic creatures,
earthly angels in this life,
for they must administer the body and the blood
of your only-begotten Son, the spotless Lamb.
(P. 2:26)

Thus, the kingdom on earth, "the way of the most holy cross" for which Catherine prays, is God's kingdom, not some grand illusion of a perfect world of her own conception.

Your Will Be Done

Central to Catherine's spiritual way is the will; at each stage of development, the will turns more to God and further away from self-will, until finally it merges with God's will. Her prayer emphasizes this interior evolution:

O most gentle love,
it seems to me you are showing
that the truest sign people are dwelling in you
is that they follow your will
not in their own way
but in your way.
This is the surest sign that people are clothed in your will
that they see the cause of events in your will
not in human will
and that they rejoice
not in material prosperity
but in adversity,
which they see as given by your will
and motivated only by your love.
(P. 2:25)

God's will for Catherine turns her toward love for her neighbor, the image of God on earth:

O fire ever blazing!
The soul who comes to know herself in you
finds your greatness wherever she turns,
even in the tiniest things,
in people
and in all created things,
for in all of them she sees
your power
and wisdom
and mercy.
(P. 12:100)

And her attitude toward her neighbor is formed by God's will:

You want us to serve you
in your way,
eternal Father,
and you guide your servants in different ways
along different paths.
And so today you show us
that we neither may nor can in any way judge
what is within a person
by the actions we see. . . .
Oh, how royally souls like this travel!
in everything
they see your will,
and so in everything your creatures do
they look for your will,
never passing judgment on the creature's intention.
(P. 9:69-70)

Give Us Bread

The bread that Catherine desires is the spiritual bread of understanding, the light of faith. This food nourishes her interior self and those for whom she prays:

So if we open the eye of our understanding
with a will to know you,
we know you,
for your light enters into every soul
who opens the gate of her will.
For the light stands at the soul's gate,
and as soon as the gate is opened to it,
the light enters,
just like the sun
that knocks at the shuttered window
and, as soon as it is opened,
comes into the house.

So the soul has to have a will to know,
and with that will
she has to open her understanding's eye,
and then you, true Sun, enter the soul
and flood her with the light that is yourself.
And once you have entered,
what do you do,
light of compassion
within the soul?
You dispel the darkness
and give her light.
(P. 15:130)

However, Catherine's prayer never could be limited to her own need; instead, she begs incessantly for the bread of mercy for all the world and especially for God's Church:

I am speaking to you,
eternal Father;
I am pleading with you,
most gracious God:
give us and all your servants
communion in the fire of your charity,
and dispose all your creatures
to receive the fruit
of the prayers and teaching
we do and must pour out
in your light and charity.
Your Truth said,
"Seek and you shall find;
ask and it shall be given to you;
knock and it shall be opened to you."
I am knocking at the door of your truth;
I am seeking and crying out
in the presence of your majesty;

> I am pleading to the ears of your clemency
> for mercy for the whole world
> and especially for holy Church.
> (P. 13:110-111)

Forgive Us as We Forgive

Love of her neighbor has so entered into Catherine's life that the gratuitous love of God animates her; forgiving and loving, she seeks no personal reward:

> She has come to know
> that she cannot love you gratuitously,
> since it is she who is obligated to you
> not you to her,
> and she has seen that this free love
> which she cannot give to you
> she must give to her neighbors,
> loving them gratuitously
> and at the same time because it is her duty.
> She loves them gratuitously
> because she does not look for a return from them,
> nor does she serve them
> for any profit she might get from them
> but only for love;
> and she loves them out of duty
> because you command it
> and it is her duty to obey you.
> (P. 11:90-91)

The gratuitous love she has received requires her to love her neighbor unconditionally:

> Eternal goodness,
> you want me to gaze into you

and see that you love me,
to see that you love me gratuitously
so that I may love everyone
with the same love.
You want me, then,
to love and serve my neighbors gratuitously,
by helping them
spiritually and materially
as much as I can,
without any expectation of selfish profit or pleasure.
Nor do you want me to hold back
because of their ingratitude or persecution,
or for any abuse I may suffer from them.
(P. 12:101-102)

Mercy and forgiveness are especially needed for the new leader of God's Church, Urban VI, a harsher and less diplomatic man than Gregory XI:

I see that you have endowed your vicar
by nature
with a fearless heart;
so I humbly, imploringly beg you
to pour the light beyond nature
into the eye of his understanding.
For unless this light,
acquired through pure affection for virtue,
is joined with it,
a heart such as his tends to be proud.
Today again let every selfish love be cut away
from these enemies of yours
and from the vicar
and from us all,
so that we may be able to forgive these enemies
when you bend their hardness.
(P. 25:217)

Deliver Us From Evil

Catherine had personally learned that struggle and temptation were necessary sufferings. Learning to endure made her less
confident of self and more reliant on divine mercy so that she
developed compassion for others. Self-doubt led her to faith in
God, to certainty that there is more to believing and trusting than
accepting what is perceived through the human sense level alone.
She prayed that others might learn this lesson:

If I look into you
I see that nothing is hid from your eyes.
Worldly people
whose eyes are blinded by the cloud of selfish love
do not see this,
for if they saw it
they would not be so cruel
to their own souls.
No,
in your compassion
they would become compassionate.
This is why we need this light —
and with all the feeling that is in me
I beg you to give this light
to all people.
(P. 15:132-133)

The only way that we can know and comprehend
any of these things
is by means of your light,
the light with which you illumine the soul's noblest aspect,
our understanding.
This light is the light of faith.
You give it to each of us Christians

> when, through the sacrament of baptism,
> you pour into us the light of your grace
> and of faith, . . .
> (P. 24:208)

Suffering caused compassion to grow in Catherine, for herself and for all others:

> What is the source of patience?
> What is the source of faith,
> of hope,
> of charity?
> The same compassion
> that gives birth to mercy.
> What frees the soul from herself
> and binds her to you?
> This compassion
> achieved in the light.
> O lovely compassion!
> O compassion,
> you are a balm
> that snuffs out rage and cruelty in the soul.
> This compassion,
> compassionate Father,
> I beg you to give to all creatures,
> especially to those you have given me
> to love with a special love.
> (P. 15:134)

Mary, The Mother of God

Catherine's *Dialogue* is dedicated to "the Name of Christ crucified and of gentle Mary" (D. 1:25); her mystical experience initiating the *Dialogue*, took place during Mass on "sweet Mary's day." Though she makes but brief mention of Mary in the *Dialogue*, these few references indicate her understanding of the integral role of Mary in the divine plan of redemption. Catherine's prayer reveals the full depth of her perception of Mary's redemptive role in the life of the Church as well as the intimacy of a personal relationship. The prayer for the feast of the Annunciation is particularly revealing as Catherine plumbs the meaning of Mary's acceptance of the angel's message. In the opening invocation Catherine's allusions expound on Mary's significance:

> Temple of the Trinity!
> O Mary, bearer of the fire!
> Mary, minister of mercy!
> Mary, seedbed of the fruit!
> Mary, redemptress of the human race —
> for the world was redeemed
> when in the Word your own flesh suffered:
> Christ
> by his passion redeemed us:
> you,
> by your grief of body and spirit.
> (P. 18:156)

Catherine identifies with her own awe and wonder at being chosen by God when she prays over Mary's response to the angel's message:

> And you were stupefied
> when you looked at yourself
> and knew how unworthy you were
> of such grace.
> So you were overtaken
> by wonder and surprise
> at the consideration of your own unworthiness
> and weakness
> and of God's unutterable grace. . . .
> it was not fear you felt
> but wonder at God's boundless goodness and charity

toward the lowliness and smallness
of your virtue.
(P. 18:158)

She sees in Mary, as in herself, the human strength, freedom,
and dignity which enable her to become a malleable instrument of
the divine Trinity: Mary is a book in which the Holy Spirit writes
the wisdom, power, and mercy of the Deity:

You, O Mary
have been made a book
in which our rule is written today.
In you today
is written the eternal Father's wisdom·
in you today
our human strength and freedom are revealed.
I say that our human dignity is revealed
because if I look at you, Mary,
I see the Holy Spirit's hand
has written the Trinity in you
by forming within you
the incarnate Word, God's only begotten Son.
He has written for us the Father's wisdom,
which this Word is;
he has written power for us,
because he was powerful enough
to accomplish this great mystery;
and he has written for us
his own — the Holy Spirit's — mercy,
for by divine grace and mercy alone
was such a great mystery
ordained and accomplished.
(P. 18:158-159)

The Catherine revealed in her mystic prayer is one who, like
her Mother Mary, responded to God with unconditional, unre-

stricted, human love. For its expression, she devised a symbolic language sufficient to convey both her own love and the consuming nature of the divine love discovered in the Godhead. This language emanated from her interior senses, transformed by love, to a refined level of affective awareness. Catherine attained the apex of affectivity, the peak point of the spiritualization of human powers.[8] From this vantage point, she enjoyed deep wisdom of herself, of the world around her, of what she could become, and of what society could achieve. In the final selection from her prayer texts, Catherine gives voice to her understanding of this transformation as she celebrates the greatness of the gift that permits her to know the things of God:

I reflect
how conformed with yourself you make the soul
when she rises up by the light of understanding
received from you true light,
and gazes upon herself
in the light of your truth
with her affection set upon you.
And then I see
that you who are God immortal
allow her to know the good things
that are immortal
and you let her enjoy them
in your charity's affection.

The reflections of Godhead which permit her to share in God's nature follow: light, fire, wisdom, and strength:

You who are light
allow her to share in the light
with you.
You who are fire
share the fire with her,
and in the fire

> you fuse your will with hers
> and hers with yours.
> You, wisdom
> give her wisdom
> to discern and recognize your truth.
> You who are strength
> give her strength,
> and she becomes so strong
> that neither demon nor any other creature
> can deprive her of your strength . . .

Finally and ultimately, in a powerful crescendo, she penetrates the mystery of partaking in the very infinity of Godhead here on earth as well as in eternal life:

> You who are infinite
> make her infinite
> by reason of the conformity you have brought about
> between yourself and her —
> by grace while she is a pilgrim in this life,
> and in everlasting life by her seeing you eternally.
> There she becomes so perfectly conformed with you
> that her free choice is enchained,
> so that she can no longer be separated from you.
> (P. 11:91-92)

Catherine speaks the language of mystic poetry that throughout all the ages, even to the present day, strains to reveal the essence of prayer that pierces the boundaries of the spirit. Her experience of love is the moving force behind her vision of the human family as united and interdependent in the mystery of God's love.

As with her conformity with the Godhead so, too, Catherine's prayer bridges the "already" and the "not yet" — the inner harmonious world of the spirit and the public world where peace and justice have yet to reign. Catherine's transformation is not a personal gift; her private interior harmony must extend beyond self to the outer public world in the continuous prayer of action, the prayer of words, and the prayer which raises her beyond the sense level. All have one purpose — to praise God and to beseech mercy for the world.

ENDNOTES

1. "It is through naming that humans progress from childhood to adulthood and learn to understand and shape the world around them." *Womanspirit Rising*, New York, 1979, p. 7.
2. Allusions to mother/child relationships do surface in Catherine's writings. She wrote to the Papal Nuncio, "what bliss for your soul, and mine, when I shall see us both bound in the fire of that divine Charity that gives her milk to suckle and nourish her children. It seems to me that this milk can only be had in the way a child draws milk and nourishment from its mother's breast." *I, Catherine*, Letter 13, p. 83. In the *Dialogue*, this image is expanded to represent the unitive stage, when the soul is gifted with spiritual calm, "an emotional union with my gentle divine nature in which she tastes milk, just as an infant when quieted rests on its mother's breast, takes her nipple, and drinks her milk through her flesh. This is how the soul who has reached this final stage rests on the breast of my divine charity and takes into the mouth of her holy desire the flesh of Christ crucified . . . how delightfully glorious is this state in which the soul enjoys such union at charity's breast that her mouth is never away from the breast nor the breast without milk." (D. 96:179-180) The Holy Spirit is "as a mother who nurses her at the breast of divine charity. . . . This servant, the Holy Spirit, whom I in my providence have given her, clothes her, nurtures her, inebriates her with tenderness and the greatest wealth." (D. 141:292) See Petroff, pp. 73-74 for an explication of this imagery common to medieval holy women.
3. *I, Catherine*, Letter 13, p. 84. Two hundred years later John of the Cross used an identical image.
4. Nicoll, p. 88.
5. *Letters*, 51, p. 155.
6. The structure of this interpretation of Catherine's prayer is based on Nicoll's exegesis of the Our Father, pp. 83-92.
7. Her consistent use of this image is seen in a letter to a young ruler, written four years earlier: "We dine at the table of the Lamb, where the Lamb himself is both our food and our servant. The Father, you see, is our table, bearing everything that is — except sin which is not in him. The Word, God's Son, has made himself our food, roasted in the blazing fire of charity, while the servant at the table is that very charity, the Holy Spirit, who gave and gives us God with his own hands. He is all the time serving us with every spiritual and temporal grace and gift." *I, Catherine*, Letter 4, p. 91.
8. Johnston, *Mirror Mind*, pp. 113-125.